Lives Given, Not Taken

21st Century Southern Baptist Martyrs

Lives Given, Not Taken

21st Century Southern Baptist Martyrs

ERICH BRIDGES
and
Jerry Rankin

Published by the International Mission Board, SBC
P.O. Box 6767
Richmond, Virginia   23230-0767

http://imb.org

Printed in the United States of America
10 09 08 07 06   2 3 4 5 6 7

ISBN: 0-9767645-3-9

Cover photography: top row: Larry and Jean Elliott; middle row: Kathy Gariety, David McDonnall, Karen Watson and Bill Koehn; bottom row: Bill Hyde and Martha Myers

To the fallen missionaries, to the co-workers who continue their task in a lost and dangerous world, to the family members left behind— and to a new generation of servants who will follow in their footsteps.

—m—

CONTENTS

ACKNOWLEDGMENTS

Many family members, current and former missionaries, friends, pastors, church members and International Mission Board staff members generously contributed their reflections, guidance, assistance, prayers, patience, encouragement—and love—to the preparation of this book. We deeply thank all of them for their help, without which this project could not have been undertaken, much less completed. Space and security considerations do not allow listing all of them. However, very special thanks go to: Lyn Hyde, Marty Koehn, Carrie McDonnall, Donna McDonnall, Jerry Gariety, Ira Myers, Gina Elliott Kim, Lorraine Neufeld, Buford and Nanci Ellis, Phil Neighbors, Keith Chase, Cliff Lea, David Hale, Shawn Macklin, Anita Bowden, Dan Allen, Sheryl Hash, Kathy Sharp, Gerry Volkart, John Brady, Carl Rees, Don Phelps, Patti Harris, Sharon Mann, Sandra Higgins and Judith Bernicchi.

WHY DO MISSIONARIES GO TO DANGEROUS PLACES?

It's not often that I'm awakened by a phone call in the middle of the night. It was 1:30 on the morning of December 30, 2002, when the shrill ringing of the telephone at my bedside startled me into a groggy semi-consciousness. Immediately the thoughts were of family. Something had happened. Something was wrong. Maybe it was my 93-year-old mother who had been in the hospital recently. Both of our children and their families were serving on the other side of the world in Asia and often forgot the radical time change that separated us, calling at strange hours to tell about the baby walking or learning new words. Our son had been detained by authorities and encountered dangerous situations numerous times in his itinerant assignment. But this wasn't a call from family.

It was the call I knew to be inevitable someday, but one I hoped would never come. A missionary had been killed; no, not one but three. Gerry Volkart, the International Mission Board's Associate Regional Leader for Northern Africa and the Middle East, informed me she had just received word that Martha Myers, Bill Koehn and Kathy Gariety had been murdered. Serving at the Jibla Baptist Hospital in Yemen, the three had been shot by an assailant as the clinic opened Monday morning. A fourth victim, a missionary pharmacist, had been wounded. Bill, the hospital's administrator, had been conferring with Kathy in his office; Martha had come in to use the phone when a gunman stepped into the doorway and opened fire, killing all three.

I fell to the floor and wept uncontrollably. The grief would have been just as severe, regardless who among our 5,400 missionary personnel had been killed. But I knew each of these personally. My mind flashed back to conversations with Martha during the previous year when she was on stateside assignment and with Kathy, who had been in the States purchasing supplies for the hospital. It had not been many years since I had visited the hospital, and my mind recalled images of the tranquil compound, the congested clinic entrance as crowds of Yemeni Arabs sought treatment in the context of a compassionate, Christian ministry from medical staff who quietly exuded a love beyond what their patients had ever experienced.

Just two weeks earlier I had been speaking at a conference, sponsored by the Evangelical Fellowship of Mission Agencies (EFMA), for personnel staff from 120 member organizations. The assigned topic was "Sending Missionaries into a Dangerous and Chaotic World," an issue that was quite relevant in the aftermath of the tragedy that had occurred on September 11, 2001. These agency leaders, responsible for enlisting and training missionary personnel, were encountering a new dimension of reticence on the part of candidates to go into a dangerous world where they would be vulnerable, not because of their Christian witness but simply because they were Americans. We all were being confronted with the challenge of equipping both new and current missionary personnel to be sensitive to matters of safety and security. The previous week Bonnie Witherall, an American missionary serving with Operation Mobilization, had been murdered in Lebanon.

A reporter attending the EFMA conference had already requested an interview following my presentation. Referencing the death of Witherall, she asked how this incident would affect our training and protection for our Southern Baptist missionaries. I elaborated on our training and the precautions our missionaries were taught to take, but in the course of my reply I was later quoted as saying, "It is not unlikely that we (the IMB) will experience such a tragedy, for no other organization has as many missionary personnel so extensively deployed and pushing to the edge of lostness." Little did I realize that two weeks later we would, indeed, experience such a tragedy.

During the previous few months a large group of our staff had been meeting for workshops on risk management and crisis response. What would we do in response to a call that someone serving with the International Mission Board was killed or kidnapped? What would be the role and responsibility of each office, and how would our response be coordinated and managed? We had dated crisis contingency plans hidden away somewhere in the files, but ever since 9/11 a renewed interest and attention had been given to these issues. The hypothetical exercises in the workshops did not fully prepare us for this early morning call and the realities we now were facing.

I thought of my first experience with this kind of news after becoming president of the IMB. From time to time missionaries have died suddenly in traffic accidents or plane crashes. It is not infrequent that illness takes the life of beloved colleagues prematurely. But on March 28, 1995, Dr. Chu Hon Yi and his wife, Kei Wol, were found strangled in their apartment in Khabarovsk, Russia. Serving an extended International Service Corps term, these Korean-Americans from Virginia Beach, Virginia, had established an effective ministry among the medical community in this far eastern city soon after the doors began to open to the former Soviet Union. I recalled the difficulty in trying to console and minister to their family and church fellowship; the answers were elusive as we tried to explain any rationale for their brutal murders.

Now, as I got dressed on the morning of December 30, CNN was already broadcasting news of unnamed American missionaries being killed by assumed terrorists in Yemen. I knew it would just be a short time until the IMB would be connected with the hospital,

"IT IS NOT UNLIKELY THAT WE (THE IMB) WILL EXPERIENCE SUCH A TRAGEDY, FOR NO OTHER ORGANIZATION HAS AS MANY MISSIONARY PERSONNEL SO EXTENSIVELY DEPLOYED AND PUSHING TO THE EDGE OF LOSTNESS."

and the calls would come. Our crisis network had already been activated. Within an hour our building was opened, security staff were in place, and overseas leadership were convening. A cadre of communications staff had arrived and was already taking calls from the media. The regional office had established direct contact with personnel in Yemen and determined official spokespersons on the scene to deal with the embassy and local investigators. Counselors and member-care staff were immediately deployed to minister to the large contingent of hospital colleagues and international staff and to assess subsequent security measures. Stateside families of the victims were notified, arrangements made for pastoral care, and families of other personnel serving in the region were called to assure them that their loved ones were safe. Meanwhile a crisis center was set up, a press conference scheduled, a phone bank manned, and hourly briefings coordinated.

There was an outpouring of support and consolation. But it did not take long for the questions to come, initially from the media, but surprisingly from missions-minded churches as well. "Why do missionaries go to dangerous places?" "How can the IMB be so irresponsible to send missionaries to places where their lives will be endangered?" There were demands to bring the missionaries home. Others reflected that this loss of life was such a waste and could have been avoided. Apparently the top priority in the minds of many was the safety of missionaries.

A little more than two months later, in March 2003, Bill Hyde, a veteran missionary who had served in the Philippines for 20 years, was killed in a terrorist bombing at the airport in Davao City. Then on March 15, 2004, five IMB personnel in Iraq were assaulted by gunmen as they drove near the city of Mosul. David McDonnall, Karen Watson, and Larry and Jean Elliott all were killed; only Carrie McDonnall survived.

It is amazing when we consider the more than 18,000 missionaries who have served with the International Mission Board throughout its almost 160-year history, that so few have met unnatural and violent deaths. Fewer than 90 have been killed, mostly in accidents. Only 29 have been murdered, many in the course of a robbery or shooting that had nothing to do with their Christian witness.

Those who give their lives in the course of service for Christ overseas are readily recognized as martyrs. Those who shed their blood do so as a witness to their faith and as a testimony to their obedience and devotion to their Lord Jesus Christ. However, some would argue with the qualifications of a martyr, insisting that only a violent and unnatural death would apply. Others would say that a martyr is only one who dies an untimely death as the direct consequence of preaching the gospel and sharing his or her faith, usually in a hostile environment.

However, most of those who hold on to the safety, comforts, and security of their American lifestyle would readily acknowledge that those who die on foreign soil because they have given of their lives as the ultimate sacrifice for the cause of Christ are martyrs. They died because of their willingness to be in a place where their lives were vulnerable; they were there because of a commitment to a higher calling than life itself. We would not quibble over the circumstances, the means of death, or the motives of those who took their lives. I am confident a martyr's crown awaits those who "did not love their life, even when faced with death" (Revelation 12:11).

Why would these missionaries and others go to places where their lives would be endangered? Why would they go to a place such as Iraq where Americans are at war and being targeted by insurgents and Muslim radicals? Why would others offer to go to places such as Afghanistan, Bosnia, the Sudan, Chechnya and serve among people who are at war and where Americans are not appreciated no matter how valued and needed their humanitarian aid? The answer is rather simple. It is because of God's call and a decision made long before to be obedient wherever He would lead. But that willingness to be obedient, even when it means risk and sacrifice, is because of the passionate conviction that Jesus is the answer for a hurting world. Missionaries in the nineteenth century did not expect to return to enjoy retirement years at home. They carried caskets as a standard part of their shipment to the field. Most of the missionaries going to West Africa died of malaria, other diseases, or violence within a few years of arrival, but they kept coming. There was a passion for their calling to take Christ to a lost world. Francis Rose, a missionary interred by the Japanese in the Philippines in 1943, reflected on colleagues who had lost their lives and believers who had died for Christ throughout the centuries with these lines:

> *Ten thousand saints come thronging home*
> *From lion's den and catacomb;*
> *The fire and sword and beasts defied;*
> *For Christ, their king, they gladly died.*

It is strange that the media do not question journalists going into war zones, traveling with troops in the midst of mortar attacks, in order to get a story, a gripping photo, or video footage for their newspaper or television network. Yet they think it foolish for others to risk their lives to bring life to those whose very existence is threatened, to give hope to those in darkness and despair, and to proclaim news of salvation to those in bondage to sin! No matter one's attitude toward war or military intervention, few would question the appropriateness, and even obligation, of troops to respond when orders come to be deployed into a war zone. An important aspect of military training for all soldiers is absolute compliance and unquestioning obedience to their commanding officer. They don't have the option of obeying orders only if it is safe to do so. They put their lives in harm's way and are willing to die for a patriotic devotion to their country and the cause of freedom. How much more should those who claim to be followers of Christ be willing to obey the orders of our supreme Commander-in-Chief who told us to go into all the world and disciple all nations?

If there is any verse of Scripture familiar to every conscientious Christian, next to John 3:16 or Psalm 23, it would be the Great Commission in Matthew 28:19-20. This command was preceded by a reminder that "all authority (had) been given to (Him) in heaven and on earth" (verse 18). Jesus had the position of authority and every right to lay claim to our lives and instruct us according to His plan and purpose. "Go, therefore and make disciples of all the nations," He said, "baptizing them in the name of the Father and the Son and the Holy Spirit, teaching them to observe all that I commanded you; and lo, I am with you always, even to the end of the age." Jesus did not qualify this mandate to go only where one could witness in safety and without risk. There was no contingency clause to disciple the nations only where one is welcomed and it is safe to do so. His passion was for the *"panta ta ethne"*—all the peoples of the world—to know Him and become His followers. He died for the whole world, but has committed the task of telling them, of proclaiming the gospel, to us, His followers.

We are reminded in Romans 10:13 that, "whoever calls on the name of the Lord shall be saved." But subsequently we are confronted with the question, "How then shall they call on Him in whom they have not believed? And how shall they believe in Him of whom they have not heard? And how shall they hear without a preacher? And how shall they preach unless they are sent? As it is written, 'How beautiful are the feet of those who preach the gospel of peace, who bring glad tidings of good things!'" (NKJV™). Why is it that 2,000 years after our Lord told us to disciple the nations, more than 4,000 ethnic-linguistic people groups, or "nations," are still identified as unreached? They have no witnessing church that is spreading the gospel in their midst, and many of them still have no Scripture in their own language.

Why is it that almost one-fourth of the world's population, approximately 1.6 billion people, have not yet heard the name of Jesus and know that He died for them? Why do missionaries go to dangerous places, take the risk and put their lives in harm's way? Because they believe that Jesus is the answer to the world's needs, and the only way for them to know is for someone to be willing to go and to share His love. "How beautiful are the feet of those who preach the gospel of peace, who bring glad tidings of good things!"

To insist that missionaries avoid the dangerous and risky places is to belittle the lostness of a world without Christ, to demean the responsibility of obedience to God's call, and to succumb to a convoluted system of values that says one's own safety and comfort is a higher priority than sharing the gospel.

The world is rather critical of those who would presume to plant their lives in a cross-cultural witness as missionaries. It is seen as being arrogant and narrow-minded to seek to convert others to one's own faith. According to contemporary detractors, missionaries are neo-colonists, infringing on traditional cultures and, out of intolerance to others' worldviews, seeking to proselytize them to embrace the Christian faith. Such shallow understanding fails to take into consideration that there is no merit whatsoever in getting someone to change from one religion to another. Counting converts or adding notches on a statistical belt would not motivate one to confront animosity and adversity for the cause of Christ. Individuals are willing to place their own lives on the line because of a conviction that Jesus Christ is the only hope of salvation and because of an awareness that those who fail to respond in repentance and faith in Him are bound for an eternal destiny in hell.

This is not just the biased opinion of narrow-minded Christians. Jesus Himself said in John 14:6, "I am the way, and the truth, and the life; no one comes to the Father but through Me." His early followers reminded both Jews and Gentiles in their testimony in Acts 4:12, "And there is salvation in no one else; for there is no other name under heaven that has been given among men, by which we must be saved." Jesus is the only, exclusive, unique way of salvation. It is not available through good works or religious ritual, regardless of the sincerity of devotion to one's cultural traditions. Only the death of Christ on the cross and His resurrection atone for the penalty of sin. There is no other way to remove the blot of sin and provide assurance of eternal life and reconciliation with a holy and righteous God. Just as Jesus was motivated by love to give His own life as a sacrifice for the sins of the world, those who go to share that good news in a lost world go, motivated by their love for God and for the people He died to save. They don't take risks out of foolish disregard for their own lives or just to get people to change their religious affiliation, but because "The love of Christ compels us" (2 Corinthians 5:14, NKJV™). There is a desperation to do whatever it takes to share Christ and His love with those who are bound for hell.

A missionary strategy coordinator was giving orientation to some new short-term personnel who had just arrived and were to be dispersed throughout a rather hostile area to witness and plant seeds of the gospel. He told them that they could be arrested for preach-

TO INSIST THAT MISSIONARIES AVOID THE DANGEROUS AND RISKY PLACES IS TO BELITTLE THE LOSTNESS OF A WORLD WITHOUT CHRIST, TO DEMEAN THE RESPONSIBILITY OF OBEDIENCE TO GOD'S CALL, AND TO SUCCUMB TO A CONVOLUTED SYSTEM OF VALUES THAT SAYS ONE'S OWN SAFETY AND COMFORT IS A HIGHER PRIORITY THAN SHARING THE GOSPEL.

ing the gospel. Then in an exhortation for boldness added, "If that happens, just be sure it's true." He explained that they would probably get deported, but it was more important for the gospel to be there than for them. Their efforts would be futile if they neglected to plant the gospel in order to guarantee their own presence and safety. This seems to be Paul's sentiments as expressed in 1 Corinthians 15:32, "If from human motives I fought with wild beasts at Ephesus, what does it profit me?" If you're going to get arrested and maybe lose your life, it might as well be for sharing the gospel! Self-preservation and personal concerns that inhibit us from proclaiming the gospel to all peoples reflect a callous disregard for those who are lost.

Those who go to places of danger do not do so reluctantly, heels dug in, conscripted into service contrary to their will. It is not a matter of the International Mission Board imposing an assignment that they are obligated to fill. Their personal relationship with Jesus Christ demands hearts of obedience in response to His redemptive grace. It is a willingness to respond to the needs of others that supersedes their own ambitions and desires. Their willingness to go is driven by a conviction that the need can be met only by going and living out their faith among the people to whom God called them.

They responded much like Isaiah in his call to go to a people in darkness. It was not so much a personal call to Isaiah as it was a generic call of God for someone to go and meet this desperate need of a rebellious people separated from Him. In Isaiah 6:8, the prophet says that he heard the voice of God saying, "Whom shall I send, and who will go for Us? ..." Isaiah did not wait for God to tap him on the shoulder and say, "You are the one!" He took initiative and asked God to send him. In essence he said, "Well, if you need someone to go to a people in darkness, let me be the one to go; I am available. Here am I. Send me!" Why was Isaiah the one to hear God's call and respond? In the earlier verses we read that Isaiah had a vision of the Lord sitting on a throne, high and exalted. He had come into a personal relationship with God and recognized that He had every right and claim on his life.

That is the motivation and calling of every missionary. They have a personal relationship with God and commitment to His Lordship that enables them to hear His call and feel the passion of His heart for a world that does not know Him. They can hear Him saying, "I have opened a door for the gospel in the communist strongholds of China, the former Soviet Union, and Eastern Europe; now, whom shall I send? I am accelerating the harvest throughout Latin America, Africa, Europe, and Asia; now, who will go for Me?

I am breaking down that last formidable barrier to global evangelization across the Muslim world of Northern Africa, the Middle East, and Central Asia; now, whom shall I send? Who will go for Me?"

Many, such as those you will read about in this book, have said, "Here am I, Lord; send me." Was it without risk? No. Was there a possibility it would cost them their lives to answer that call? Yes. Did they know that sacrifice and suffering would be the cost? There was no question. But they went joyfully and willingly, rejoicing in the privilege of being among those chosen to bring salvation to those who had not known and were deprived of knowing Jesus. Like their Savior, who, "… for the joy set before Him, endured the cross, despising the shame …" (Hebrews 12:2), they were willing to die for the sake of salvation being extended to a people and nation.

Those whose lives we honor and celebrate in this volume knew the risk involved. They had been thoroughly trained in matters related to security and safety, but there was something more important, more compelling, than self-preservation. They had discovered that there was something worth living for, something worth giving their lives for, and, yes, something worth dying for. Paul described it as the high calling of God. Obedience to God's call and the opportunity to minister to the needs of people who were hopeless and in despair was worth the risk.

After Bill, Martha and Kathy were killed in Yemen, it often was said that the gunman did not take their lives on that morning, for he could not take from them what they had already given. Jesus had made His call clear to His disciples in Matthew 16:24. He said, "If anyone wishes to come after Me, he must deny himself, and take up his cross and follow Me." The call to follow Christ was a call to die.

The call to discipleship and obedience always has been one to deny self, to die to one's own ambitions and forgo self-preservation. Jesus has never changed the missionary call and conditions for following Him. Indeed, the calling to anyone who would be His disciple is one of sacrifice and a willingness to lay down one's life.

THERE WAS SOMETHING MORE IMPORTANT, MORE COMPELLING, THAN SELF-PRESERVATION. THEY HAD DISCOVERED THAT THERE WAS SOMETHING WORTH LIVING FOR, SOMETHING WORTH GIVING THEIR LIVES FOR, AND, YES, SOMETHING WORTH DYING FOR.

So Bill Koehn, Martha Myers, Kathy Gariety and others did not die when their lives were suddenly ended by an assassin's bullet or a terrorist bomb; they had died to self when they trusted Jesus as their Savior years ago. When all of them left promising business and medical careers in the States to go as missionaries to Yemen, they gave their lives and died. Each day they served the Lord in Yemen, healing the sick, ministering to orphans, widows and prisoners, they had to lay their lives on the altar and die. They knew the risk. As hospital administrator, Bill had been threatened many times. Martha had already been kidnapped. They knew they might not live to retirement and had made arrangements for their bodies to be buried in Yemen.

As I knelt and wept at their graves on the backside of the hospital compound a few weeks after their deaths, I thought of the testimony of Bill's son-in-law at his memorial service in Texas. He put this tragedy into a kingdom perspective as he reflected on the 28 years Bill and his wife, Marty, had given themselves to the people of Yemen. He said, "Sometime in the future, a Yemeni Arab man will be walking hand-in-hand with his son up a hillside in Jibla and will come across a crude grave marker. After a pause, the man will say, 'Son, this is the man that brought Jesus to our people.'"

Tertullian was the ancient church father who said, "The blood of martyrs is the seed of the church." Rather than a defeat for the kingdom, blood that is spilled as a life witness has the power to give authenticity to the gospel. Already there is evidence that many in the community who were benefactors of the compassionate medical care they found at Jibla Baptist Hospital have begun to consider the claims of Christ. Those who silently observed and evaluated the faith that motivated these American missionaries to come to such a remote location have begun to consider the validity of their witness. Once they saw it was something these missionaries considered worth giving their lives for, they, too, began to embrace the truth of the gospel. The faithful obedience and witness through the lives of Bill, Martha, Kathy, and others, were simply preparation for what God will do through their deaths.

One day there will be a multitude from every tribe, people, tongue, and nation represented around the throne of God. There will be Yemeni Arabs, Iraqis, Kurds, and Filipinos among that multitude because of many who were willing to give their lives in faithful obedience. Reaching all peoples for Christ will not be accomplished without the blood of martyrs. That is not our strategy, and it is never intentional. We give high priority to providing security for missionary personnel and their families. But Jesus sent His disciples into a hostile environment to share the gospel and demonstrated the cost by giving His own life on the cross. We must not think that the call to take up our cross and die was only for those in the first century. It will always be the cost for reaching our world for Christ.

In His final instructions to His disciples, Jesus reminded them that they would be hated and persecuted just as He had been, because a slave was not greater than his master. They were not to be of this world, and therefore the world would hate them. In fact, Jesus added, "… An hour is coming for everyone who kills you to think that he is offering service to God. These things they will do, because they have not known the Father or Me" (John 16:2-3). The answer to why people are killed and missionaries are martyred is very simple. It is not because of lack of security, flaws in international relations, or insensitivity to diverse and conflicting worldviews. It is because of a sinful and fallen world that does not know God. It is the reason suicide bombers can believe they are serving God by destroying themselves and innocent lives. Terrorists can be deluded into thinking they gain eternal merit by acts of hatred and destruction because they do not know God and His redemptive love through Jesus Christ. Rather than threats and dangers causing us to withdraw and cower in fear, they should compel us to go and confront a sinful world with the life-changing power of the gospel.

Following 9/11, about 100 missionary families were temporarily relocated from their place of assignment. This normally would be a decision made by overseas personnel since they are on the scene and in the best position to assess the need for evacuation. However, knowing that there likely would be an immediate American military response to this terrorist attack, realizing the potential backlash from Muslim populations anywhere in the world and knowing that we were not dealing with a local threat or conflict, the decision was made for those in the most vulnerable places to move to a safer environment. The negative reaction on the part of these missionaries

WE MUST NOT THINK THAT THE CALL TO TAKE UP OUR CROSS AND DIE WAS ONLY FOR THOSE IN THE FIRST CENTURY. IT WILL ALWAYS BE THE COST FOR REACHING OUR WORLD FOR CHRIST.

was overwhelming; they were not concerned for their own safety, but for the needs of "their people" whom they were having to leave behind.

More recently, in a volatile area of the world that was experiencing an attempt to overthrow the government, the State Department issued an advisory that all non-essential U.S. citizens should evacuate. There were demonstrations in the streets and anarchy prevailed. Parents of missionaries serving in that country were monitoring the situation and expected their children to come home in response to this notice. But the missionaries replied that they would not be leaving for three reasons: (1) We are "essential" personnel! (2) God has called us to this country, and we cannot be disobedient to His call out of regard for our own safety. (3) It is times such as this when the chaos and uncertainties in society create the greatest openness to spiritual answers. We cannot abandon the people at what may be our greatest opportunity for witness!

The appeal to bring missionaries home from places of danger is usually based on an egocentric perspective in which one's own comfort and security is the highest value and priority. The relativism of post-modern thinking would deny that there is a truth worth living and dying for. Both attitudes are blatant contradictions of the call to discipleship.

In the 1980s when Muslim radicals had thrown Lebanon into chaos and a protracted civil war, and Americans, such as Terry Waite, were being kidnapped, there was a mandate that all U.S. citizens withdraw. Those who refused had their passports canceled and were considered in contempt of law. Reluctantly, missionaries evacuated to Cyprus.

The following summer one of those missionaries, Frances Fuller, gave a testimony at Missions Week at Ridgecrest Baptist Assembly in North Carolina and thanked Southern Baptists for their prayers. She said, "Because of your prayers I am here tonight." There was a massive, standing ovation in response. Then Frances continued, "But you don't understand. I am here because you prayed the wrong prayer. You were praying that we would be safe and could get out of Lebanon. The missionaries were praying that we would be permitted to stay and continue our ministries. The people to whom God called us were not able to leave; they remain behind and suffer alone. But because there are more of you than there were of us, your prayers prevailed."

I don't know about the theological validity of the volume of prayer affecting the outcome, but Frances was correct in acknowledging our misdirected prayers. Certainly we should be concerned about our own safety and that of our missionaries around the world, but our greater concern should be that the gospel would be made known and God would be glorified, whether by life or by death.

An unwillingness to suffer or entail risk implies a conditional commitment that definitely inhibits what God is able to do through us. Even missionaries draw a bottom line that is short of total surrender because they come out of an American culture of entitlement that views safety, health, and security as fundamental rights. One missionary, speaking to colleagues, reminded them that they were to view life through the lens of eternity in which they, like Paul, view suffering as "momentary light affliction," and that "suffering is not worthy to be compared with the glory that is to be revealed." He challenged the assumption that we have a right to be comfortable. Acknowledging the dangers of life on the mission field, he reminded his audience that the call to the ministry is not a call to comfort, safety, and self-indulgence, as our American culture would have us believe. Most of the world knows this, and we need to recognize that any comfort or safety we happen to enjoy is a blessing, not a right.

Americans were indignant when terrorists flew planes into the Pentagon and the World Trade Center on September 11, 2001, but the reality is that we were now subjected to what most of the world has always experienced. It is right that we should grieve when missionaries are killed, but the reality is that thousands of Christians die for their faith throughout the world every year. They do not have an American passport that will allow them to escape the threats and dangers in which they live every day. No international agency stands poised to rush to their defense. So Christian believers are massacred in villages across Indonesia, arrested in China and Vietnam, and countless numbers disappear throughout the Muslim world. Is not our faith worth dying for as much as that of those of national Christians who live every day with the possibility it may be their last? We are challenged by the second verse of the hymn, "Am I a Soldier of the Cross," which says:

> *Must I be carried to the skies*
> *On flowery beds of ease,*
> *While others fought to win the prize,*
> *And sailed through bloody seas?*

We are reminded in 1 Peter 2:21, "For you have been called for this purpose, since Christ also suffered for you, leaving you an example for you to follow in His steps." In Chapter 4, verses 12 and 13, the thought continues, "Beloved, do not be surprised at the fiery ordeal among you, which comes upon you for your testing, as though some strange thing were happening to you; but to the degree that you share the sufferings of Christ, keep on rejoicing, so that also at

AN UNWILLINGNESS TO SUFFER OR ENTAIL RISK IMPLIES A CONDITIONAL COMMITMENT THAT DEFINITELY INHIBITS WHAT GOD IS ABLE TO DO THROUGH US.

the revelation of His glory, you may rejoice with exultation." James 1:2 echoes the same theme, "Consider it all joy, my brethren, when you encounter various trials." That doesn't reflect the typical American mindset that would say to avoid suffering, eschew potential trials, and choose the easy and comfortable lifestyle. Most of the world knows suffering and deprivation, but sadly they never know of the hope eternity can offer because we are unwilling to risk our lives and identify with their suffering. To consider one's physical existence to be of supreme value fits the thinking of an atheist or communist who embraces materialism and earthly existence as the ultimate good in life. But it makes no sense whatsoever to a Christian who is committed to the kingdom of God and eternal values.

If safety is to be the criterion for missionary service, where does one serve? It would certainly not be anywhere in the Muslim world where antagonistic fanatics and suicide bombers are a threat. Anti-Christian sentiments are still rampant in communist countries and extremism is growing daily among Hindu radicals in India. Conditions are unhealthy in Africa, and Latin America teems with drug gangs and guerrilla groups who kidnap foreigners for ransom. That leaves Europe, Australia, and North America, but all have been victims of terrorist bombings in recent years. If self-concerns for comfort and security are the determining factors for whether or not the gospel is shared, then we can forget the Great Commission, cease our involvement in international missions, and bring the missionaries home!

We readily forget that the sacrifice of one's life is one of the most powerful tools in God's spiritual armament for extending the kingdom to the ends of the earth. Immediately after the death of our missionaries in Yemen, another organization lost personnel in Somalia. A short time later Martin Burnham was killed in the Philippines after being held hostage by the Abu Shaaf guerrillas with his wife, Gracia, for more than a year. Confirmation of the deaths of three missionaries with New Tribes Mission, kidnapped years earlier in Panama and killed in the jungles of Colombia, had come only the year before. Colombia was where IMB missionary Charlie Hood was gunned down in the driveway of his home a few years earlier.

Every day there are national believers who are martyred, and the cost of following Christ is their lives. Why is the gospel flourishing in China? Before new believers are baptized they are asked if they will faithfully follow Christ even when the authorities drag them out of their homes, confiscate their belongings, threaten their

> TO CONSIDER ONE'S PHYSICAL EXISTENCE TO BE OF SUPREME VALUE FITS THE THINKING OF AN ATHEIST OR COMMUNIST WHO EMBRACES MATERIALISM AND EARTHLY EXISTENCE AS THE ULTIMATE GOOD IN LIFE.

families, and throw them in jail. They are taught to say when possibly sentenced to death, "You do not take my life from me, but I offer it freely to you as a testimony of faith in Jesus Christ who loved me and gave His life for me." How can the witness of the church be deterred by threats and suffering in the face of that kind of attitude? The possibility of death is inconsequential for believers who already dealt with it when they came to faith and chose to be followers of Jesus Christ.

Joseph Tson, a Baptist leader in Romania during the communist rule of the 1970s, told of being arrested. When he refused to cooperate and comply with the request of the authorities to cease preaching, they threatened to kill him. The officer said, "Don't you realize I have the power to take your life?" Joseph Tson replied, "I am more powerful than you, for I have the power to lay down my life for what I believe; you cannot take it from me!" He smiled and continued, "If you kill me, you send me to glory; that's no threat, in fact, that is my ultimate desire. The more I suffer here, the greater the glory up there." He discovered the secret expressed by the Apostle Paul, "For to me, to live is Christ and to die is gain" (Philippians 1:21). Dietrich Bonhoffer, before he died in a Nazi concentration camp, expressed his understanding of the call of Christ, "The call to discipleship is a call to die."

The stories and testimonies you will read in the following chapters are of those who answered that call. They did not anticipate their lives being ended prematurely as we would consider it from our perspective. They still had goals and plans for their work and ministry in the days to follow; they had dreams and visions of reaching the people to whom God had called them. But they could say with Paul, "I have fought the good fight, I have finished the course, I have kept the faith; … there is laid up for me the crown of righteousness, which the Lord … will award to me on that day" (2 Timothy 4:7-8). Their lives were not taken from them, for they had already given them!

—Jerry Rankin

YEMEN PROLOGUE

It was Southern Baptists' 9/11.

Not just in its deadliness and its harsh message that the world had become more dangerous—but in its terrible quickness and finality.

It came in a single burst of violence on the morning of December 30, 2002. A Muslim militant in Yemen—enraged by the influence of Christian ministry in his land, and in his own family—shot and killed Southern Baptist medical missionaries Bill Koehn, Martha Myers, and Kathy Gariety, seriously wounding pharmacist Don Caswell.

Ironically, it was the last day of Jibla Baptist Hospital's regular operation before a long-negotiated transfer to Yemeni administration. Abed Abdul Razak Kamel arrived early that morning. He held a "pink slip" pass for return patients, which allowed him past hospital security guards into the outpatient waiting area.

He sat there, quietly—and waited.

At 8:15, Martha Myers walked past him into Bill Koehn's office, where Kathy Gariety was already sitting. Kamel followed her, pulled out a pistol hidden under his coat—and opened fire on the three workers at point-blank range.

As hospital workers screamed and scattered, Kamel emerged from the office, walked to the pharmacy, and shot Don Caswell three times. Two Yemeni soldiers at the front gate heard the shots and commotion, ran into the courtyard, and confronted Kamel. He calmly laid his gun on the ground and raised his hands.

Bill Koehn had led the hospital as administrator for 28 years, guiding hundreds of employees and medical staff through countless crises.

"Dr. Martha" had treated and befriended thousands of Yemenis—including Kamel's wife—for more than 20 years. Kathy Gariety had expertly managed the hospital's supply operation for 10 years, ministering in her free time to hospital staff and local families.

All those years. All those relationships. Three remarkable lives—ended, snuffed out in a few moments.

Or so the killer thought …

BILL KOEHN

quiet giant

Bill Koehn

On the morning he was shot, Bill Koehn was working at his desk—as usual.

When they found him, mortally wounded, he sat slumped in his chair. Co-workers Martha Myers and Kathy Gariety lay on the floor nearby—one dead, the other dying. Chaos and confusion still reigned outside on a hospital compound terrorized by a shooting rampage.

But inside Bill's office, where gunshots had exploded minutes before, a strange and holy quiet had descended.

They rushed Bill and Kathy on gurneys to the main hospital. Southern Baptist surgeon Judy Williams saw immediately that Bill's

> "I PUT MY HEAD ON HIS CHEST AND
> CRIED LIKE A BABY..."

wounds were fatal. She did what she could for Kathy, who soon died in one of the operating rooms. Judy and another surgeon focused on pharmacist Don Caswell, who had been shot three times but was stable and conscious.

Nurse Kaye Rock cared for Bill as his life ebbed away. "I put my head on his chest and cried like a baby," she said.

Marty Koehn, Bill's wife of 39 years, soon came in. She stood beside him, comforted him, and held his rough carpenter's hand.

In a few minutes, he was gone.

Bill had been handling details that morning. It was Jibla Baptist Hospital's last day of operation; after long negotiations, a Yemeni government charity was set to take over control from the International Mission Board.

He had a heavy heart about the transition after a quarter-century of guiding the busy hospital as administrator. And he was tired. The years and countless hospital crises had taken a toll. Too much work, too many needs and patients, too few doctors and nurses to meet them. He was 60 and anticipated early retirement in less than a year.

"I just want to leave with honor," he had confided to a colleague during an earlier crisis.

But he was on the job that morning, like every morning, taking care of business.

That was Bill Koehn. Taking care of business—with honor—up to his final moments.

"Integrity" is a word you hear again and again when friends and family talk about this quiet man from Kansas. Not the malleable, negotiable sort seen so often these days, even in Christian circles. Bill had the kind of integrity defined by Webster: "an uncompromising adherence to a code of moral values; utter sincerity, honesty, and candor; avoidance of deception, expediency, artificiality or shallowness of any kind ..."

Bill was old school. He worked hard. He did things right the first time. He did the right thing. If he made a promise, it was kept.

Unfinished projects, whether at the hospital or in his woodworking shop, irked him.

> BILL WAS OLD SCHOOL. HE WORKED HARD.
> HE DID THINGS RIGHT THE FIRST TIME.
> HE DID THE RIGHT THING.

He told the truth, the whole truth, and nothing but the truth—even when it cost him. He treated others with patience and generosity, but was hard on himself.

"I thought I was a man of integrity—until I met Bill," admits a long-time co-worker.

According to his son-in-law, Randal Pearce, Bill was "what a Midwestern man is supposed to be: hardworking, direct, straightforward, kind, and loving."

Well into his adult life, however, Bill had no notion or desire to be a missionary. He was a grocer—and a good one. He'd worked his way up from stocker to store manager. He had a good job, a loving Christian wife, two energetic little daughters. He could have spent a long, contented life managing his store, being a husband and father, serving in his church, staying close to home.

Then God came to call. And Bill found that real contentment comes from following Him wherever He leads.

But it took awhile—and some divine persuasion.

William Edwin Koehn (pronounced "KANE") was born and raised in Cimarron, Kansas, a small county seat town on the old Santa Fe Trail that once led wagon trains west. He was the seventh of seven children; elder son David and baby Bill were bookends for a row of five daughters.

"I was loved and cared for lavishly, since I was a boy after five straight girls," he once said, fondly looking back on childhood.

But he wasn't spoiled. Work and responsibility entered the picture early for this son of a shoe and canvas repairman. Early jobs included a newspaper route (50 customers), yard work for town folk, helping his father after school at the repair shop. He worked throughout high school, but managed to find time for basketball, track, and choir.

"Bill had a strong work ethic, largely instilled in him by his parents and his older brother, Dave," says Marty Koehn. "It meant that when he had a mild sickness for which he might have gotten sick leave, he went to work anyway. If he was sick enough to miss work, he didn't allow himself to go out to his carpentry shop, even if he felt better after resting."

Bill accepted Christ as Savior when he was 8 years old, during a revival meeting held by the Southern Baptist mission church in Cimarron. He experienced the power of God's grace—and the beginnings of a lifelong desire to please Him.

"The thing I remember most about my salvation was my release from guilt—and a change in my motive for behavior," he later observed. "I tried to behave properly because I knew that was what Christ expected of a Christian."

It was the simple approach to practical faith God expects of us all. Many of us start out with it—but lose it amid the pressures and distractions of life. Bill never lost it.

Bill learned construction and carpentry while building houses with his brother during summers and after high school. He entered the University of Kansas at Lawrence in the fall of 1960 and got involved with the Baptist Student Union. One ministry opportunity attracted his especially enthusiastic commitment: serving as a taxi service for college girls needing rides to church. When he was a junior, he began dating a young coed named Marty Walker.

"As we dated, we both sought the Lord's will about choosing a life partner, and God confirmed what we were already sensing," Marty recalls.

They were married in September 1963. Bill left school to work construction with his brother, but the bottom fell out of the building market in Kansas that year. He signed on with a plumbing company and learned all about sewers and Roto-rooters, but that company soon went out of business, too. So Bill got a job sacking groceries at the Ideal Food Store in Liberal, Kansas. His new career was born.

Within six years, Bill's work ethic got him promoted from sacker to stocker, head stocker, assistant manager—and finally manager at a large Ideal store in Hays, Kansas. Marty finished college. Their two daughters, Janelda ("Jay") and Samantha, were born in 1964 and 1971. Wherever they moved with Bill's work, the Koehns sought out Southern Baptist churches and grew in the Lord.

In 1966, a local pastor's wife paid for Marty's travel to Foreign Missions Week at Glorieta (New Mexico) Baptist Conference Center. During the week, she felt God renew a call to missions she had first sensed as a child—and she responded in obedience.

"I returned home to Bill and told him about the commitment I had made," she recounts. "He was decidedly not interested in going to the foreign mission field, but he let me begin working on meeting the educational requirements for missionary appointment.

"He basically humored me. After all, what harm could that do?"

Whenever a Foreign Mission Board personnel representative came to visit at Marty's invitation, she would enthusiastically ask questions about potential service. Bill would sit back and listen—strictly noncommittal.

"HE WAS DECIDEDLY NOT INTERESTED IN
GOING TO THE FOREIGN MISSION FIELD…"

"Then he would walk the representative to the car and tell him we weren't going to be missionaries and that they were wasting their time coming to see us," Marty says. "It was a source of some tension between us, but we just waited on the Lord to see what He would do."

Bill wasn't hostile toward missions. He just couldn't see himself as a missionary. He had no sense of call and didn't try to hide the fact.

"I rejected the idea completely, and continued to plan my advancement in the grocery business," he wrote of the time.

But he did agree to go with Marty to Foreign Missions Week the next year—and the year after that. The wall of resistance began to show some cracks.

"I could see the need and the possibility that I had a talent God could use"—business management—in missions, he grudgingly admitted to himself. "I decided to say neither yes nor no, but to begin to earnestly seek God's will."

By 1973, God's direction was clear. When he surrendered himself to it, Bill said he experienced "an ease and contentment in my life that I had not felt in many years."

Once the inward struggle was resolved, Bill made a major outward sacrifice—and took a giant step of faith—to seal his commitment. It was a risky move for a family man with three other lives depending on his earning power.

To meet requirements for missionary appointment as a business manager, he had to finish college (and later attend seminary for a time). To have time for study, he knew he had to give up his store management position, just as he was entering what would have been his prime years in the business. He swallowed hard and asked for a demotion.

He went back to stocking shelves—in the same store where he'd been the boss for two years. It was an act of humility, a quality he would model many times in years to come.

"When he took the demotion, some people saw the action as foolish," Marty remembers. "But they respected him for working towards a goal."

The goal: God's service. The destination: a Baptist mission hospital in a tiny village called Jibla, in an isolated Arab nation called Yemen. It needed a business manager. Bill had never considered hospital administration, but he knew how to manage people and keep a busy enterprise running.

"From all I have learned, it seems to be just the place I have been trained for thus far in life," he earnestly wrote in 1974, the year he and Marty were appointed Southern Baptist missionaries.

He had no idea how prophetic his words would prove to be.

SMALL CITY, LITTLE WORLD

A hospital is a small city, a little world unto itself.

It has employees and customers, residents and visitors, joys and sorrows, the sick and the well, the living and dying, the young and the old—and at least one crisis a week. A hospital must have medical professionals to perform its mission, but it cannot function without a "mayor."

That was Bill's role as business manager and administrator.

Perhaps "father" is a better analogy. It's one Bill would have preferred, at any rate; he was far too honest to be a politician. He became a father to the Jibla Baptist Hospital family. Not the "great white father" of missionary stereotype. Not the "founding father" of the hospital—that was James Young, the missionary doctor who started the institution in 1967. Bill would be the gentle father figure so many in and around Jibla needed.

Once they got to know him, "all the Yemenis referred to Bill as their father," Marty observes. "They still do. He was loved and respected by all, probably because he kept his word."

It was a big job from the beginning.

Imagine managing a hospital for the first time, learning as you go, making major decisions almost daily—while struggling to learn a new language, new customs, a strange new culture. New to you, at least, but historically ancient and bound to tribal and Islamic traditions. To keep the hospital running, you must quickly grasp not only its many inner workings but all those cultural quirks.

That was Bill's challenge, and it only grew larger through the years. The hospital expanded to 90 beds, handled hundreds of surgeries each month and served as many as 40,000 patients a year in the wards and the busy outpatient clinic. They came from throughout the country, like pilgrims, because of Jibla's reputation for high-quality, compassionate care.

The workload was endless. But Bill started his tenure—and each day—with little acts of kindness.

While still studying Arabic full time their first year in Yemen, the Koehns spent several afternoons a week supervising poor village women allowed to enter the hospital compound. The women used short sickles to cut grass for their animals to eat. The swinging sickle blades often became too dull to cut much grass, but they still sliced the women's hands quite effectively.

"Bill noticed that very quickly," Marty recalls. "He encouraged them to wash out the wounds immediately and gave them Band-Aids to keep them clean."

The women stood amazed. They were unaccustomed to being acknowledged by any man, much less a powerful foreigner.

Another service Bill introduced early on: He attached faucets to the hospital water tanks that reached outside the compound fence—enabling villagers with no running water to fill their jugs without pleading permission for entry. The silent ministry continues today.

"Countless cups of water have been given in Jesus' name in this way," Marty says.

When he took up full administrative duties, Bill faced the daily task of directing an ever-changing cast of nearly 200 hospital workers. Southern Baptist doctors and nurses. Medical professionals from many other countries and agencies. Long- and short-term contract workers. Local Yemeni workers. Medical staff. Administrative staff. Kitchen staff. Maintenance and repair workers.

Bill made a daily routine of greeting every worker he encountered and shaking hands. He knew each name, each face. He even recognized the individual voices of veiled Muslim women workers—and greeted them by name, too. When he handed out wages on payday, he made it a point to reach across his desk to grasp a hand and thank each worker for helping the hospital continue to serve.

Daily routines were vitally important to Bill. He was a man of discipline and a creature of habit—traits that probably helped him maintain sanity when things got crazy at Jibla.

Each day started with Bible reading and prayer. For many years he read through Christ's Sermon on the Mount daily and meditated on it as a pattern for living.

Every morning he emerged before 6 a.m. and walked from his little duplex on the compound to the hospital. There, using a simple system he devised, he distributed numbered tickets to Yemenis— sometimes 20, sometimes 100 or more—waiting to see a doctor at the outpatient clinic. Many had been there since 4 a.m., or had camped out all night.

Morning chapel time was 6:30. At 7 a.m. Bill returned to check the clinic, make sure patient rounds were proceeding on the wards and verify that visitors had cards allowing hospital entry. At 7:55 he went to eat breakfast. Back at 8:30, he occupied the "cashier's box" until noon, collecting (or trying to collect) payment from departing patients, handling other financial matters, dealing with patients' families. At noon, lunch.

In the afternoon, as the clinic began to wind down, Bill usually supervised the cashier's box once again, audited receipts, closed the clinic at 2 p.m. and locked cash in the safe. He went home around 3, rested for an hour or so, then re-emerged to work in the little carpentry shop made of old shipping crates next to his house. At 6, Bill and Marty sat down to eat. From 7 to 9 p.m. they might watch a video or CNN (the compound had a satellite dish in later years).

> "YOU NEVER CALLED BILL AFTER 9,
> BECAUSE HE WAS IN BED. HE WAS
> VERY STRUCTURED."

After that, lights out.

"You never called Bill after 9, because he was in bed," says a long-time colleague. "He was very structured."

Still, he never really escaped the hospital's reach. If emergencies or complaints arose, Bill lived only 50 yards away on the compound. He and Marty also kept the hospital's books. He paid all employees and handled the hiring of everyone from the doctors to the cooks. A trusted Yemeni associate helped him in many ways, but the buck stopped with Bill.

"I can't think of another man who could have handled the administrative nightmares that Bill did," says the colleague, still awed by the feat. "I speak from experience, because I was administrator when Bill was gone (on U.S. assignment). I barely made it a year. I lost it over and over again. I would raise my voice; I'd get totally frustrated."

Yemenis, like many peoples of the Middle East, relish protracted bargaining over everything—including medical bills. The custom comes from a long and rich history of street markets, bazaars, and trade routes. To them, Jibla's supposedly set prices were only starting points for negotiation. For many poor families who made perhaps $500 in a good year, it might be the largest expense of a lifetime.

One day his frustrated co-worker asked Bill, "How in the world do you do this?"

"I'll ask for payment two or three times," Bill explained. "And when I feel my temperature rising, I'll say, 'C'mon, let's go into town, and I'll buy you a cup of tea.'"

That simple, human gesture would usually break the ice—and pave the way for agreement.

Jibla was a Christian mission hospital in the heart of one of the region's poorest countries. It never turned anyone away who needed treatment because of lack of funds. But it needed paying customers to continue operation.

Those conflicting priorities weighed more and more heavily on Bill through the years. As expenses, inflation and patient loads in creased, so did the financial pressures. By the early 1990s the hospital cost more than $1 million a year to run. Only about half of that total came from the International Mission Board.

But Bill rarely lost sight of the bigger picture—the one seen through God's eyes. The hospital existed to minister to people in Jesus' name. And people came first.

Once, a sick man in need of surgery hired a truck to take him on the six-hour journey to Jibla. On the way his money was stolen, but the hospital cared for him anyway. When he recovered and returned home, he sold his cow to pay the bill.

A woman, seven months pregnant, was clearing a steep slope when a large rock crushed her leg. At the first hospital where she was taken, doctors told her they would have to amputate the leg.

"No!" she cried in desperation. "Take me to Jibla."

After Martha Myers surgically repaired her leg, the woman gave birth to a healthy child—and walked home three months later. The hospital absorbed most of the costs for her stay.

Even a man who had feuded with the hospital—after Bill took legal action to move him off hospital-owned property where he had squatted for years—returned in his hour of need. When his son was ill and dying, the man brought him to the hospital.

"Deep down inside they knew we cared and we loved them and we'd do the best for them," says a former hospital worker.

It didn't always sit well with other medical institutions in Yemen when so many Yemenis bypassed them—riding or walking for days to seek out the little Baptist hospital in isolated Ibb Province. This, moreover, in a staunchly Muslim land that had no known Christian witness for some 1,300 years before Jibla opened.

But word had spread: They treat you like a human being there, regardless of who you are or where you come from. Jibla had that reputation from its beginning. Bill nurtured and greatly enlarged it on his watch.

"He treated the rich and the poor with respect," says a friend and admirer. "He knew how to culturally honor government and tribal officials who came into his office, and he had a deep sense of responsibility for those in his charge—whether it was a Yemeni worker who cleaned bathrooms or a highly trained European surgeon."

The esteem Yemenis returned to him was powerfully illustrated when a regional sheik invited Bill to an event honoring the U.S. ambassador to Yemen. As a sign of his regard for the hospital and its leader, the sheik insisted that Bill head the procession and that the top

American VIP in the nation follow behind. The ambassador was duly humbled—and Bill duly embarrassed. But the sheik made his point.

"HE HAD A DEEP SENSE OF RESPONSIBILITY FOR THOSE IN HIS CHARGE—WHETHER IT WAS A YEMENI WORKER WHO CLEANED BATHROOMS OR A HIGHLY TRAINED EUROPEAN SURGEON."

Mutual respect marked relationships between Bill and his staff at every level. Building on what he learned managing people back in Kansas, he used positive motivation—not a heavy hand. He looked for potential to encourage, emphasized people's strengths, and patiently helped them overcome weaknesses.

"He always attempted to teach employees who were not performing well in their jobs," Marty recalls. "He showed them how to improve so they could keep their jobs, rather than firing them for small errors."

The hospital, after all, was the top employer in the area. Many Jibla families depended on jobs there to put food in their children's mouths. But Bill's approach went beyond competent management.

"He cared very deeply for his workers," says surgeon Judy Williams.

"It didn't matter if it was Yemeni workers, international workers, whoever, he cared for them all, for their families—and for the patients the hospital served."

He was an expert at conflict management, which was essential in a place where so many lives intersected in high-stress situations.

"Don't say anything the first year," he wisely advised new international workers before they protested hospital procedures or bewildering local customs.

He was the boss, but he led quietly. When he spoke, he said something worth listening to.

> "I'VE HEARD MEEKNESS DEFINED AS 'STRENGTH UNDER CONTROL.' IF THAT IS TRUE, THE MOST ACCURATE PICTURE I CAN THINK OF WOULD BE MR. BILL."

"I've heard meekness defined as 'strength under control,'" says a Southern Baptist nurse who observed Bill in action. "If that is true, the most accurate picture I can think of would be Mr. Bill. He knew when to be democratic and when to step in and provide authority. Having been in Yemen the longest, he was the expert in our eyes— but he wouldn't offer an opinion unless asked. His preferred place in church was in the back row near the door."

When push came to shove, however, Bill could handle confrontation. He met it with his preferred weapon: truth.

During one especially difficult time when the hospital was being falsely accused of abetting a crime, the threat of closure loomed. Bill calmly submitted to seven straight hours of questioning by the police. The crisis passed.

On another occasion, he was negotiating with the government about a crucial issue. A lawyer for the hospital urged him, "Don't tell them the whole truth all at once. Give them a little bit at a time." Bill rejected the advice and stated his case clearly and completely.

"Bill always carefully chose his words to be accurate," explains a friend. "This was something the Yemenis were shocked by, time and time again. In a society where truth is relative, he worked hard to get the facts straight and present the story accurately the first time. The Yemenis would keep waiting for the 'real truth' to surface and would be flabbergasted that this man had presented the real truth—in its entirety—in the first place."

Another time, a barren woman, who desperately wanted a baby, slipped into the hospital and stole a newborn from the maternity ward. The police came to investigate and questioned hospital workers. No one person on staff was obviously to blame for negligence in the incident, but custom demanded that someone be punished.

The police asked Bill to name who was responsible. He refused; he didn't know if anyone deserved blame. The authorities threatened to arrest one of the Yemeni workers anyway.

"Arrest me instead," Bill responded. After all, he was ultimately responsible for everything that happened on hospital grounds.

"They didn't take him up on the offer, for which we were all grateful," Marty admits.

TOYS, ORPHANS, AND WIDOWS

As dedicated as he was, even Bill needed a mental break from the daily grind. He found it in his little woodworking shop—a sanctuary from the problems and demands of his job.

"It was his release," says a friend.

Through Bill's skilled hands, however, God turned a hobby into a blessing for the people of Yemen. It started with furniture for the hospital—bedside tables for patients, lockers for the new staff dressing room. He spent his own money on the projects, bought his own wood.

> "THE NICE PART ABOUT MAKING TOYS IS THAT YOU CAN GIVE THEM TO CHILDREN WHO DON'T REALLY HAVE MANY TOYS HERE. SOMETIMES WHEN CHILDREN COME IN AND THEY'RE FRIGHTENED, A TOY EASES ADMISSION TO THE HOSPITAL."

Then he noticed that a wooden toy did wonders to calm the fears of a sick child coming into the big, scary hospital. He fashioned little cars, trucks, airplanes, and other creations for young patients.

"The nice part about making toys is that you can give them to children who don't really have many toys here," Bill reflected. "Most of the toys go to the nurses' station; there's a box there for the children. Sometimes when children come in and they're frightened, a toy eases admission to the hospital."

Ever practical, he even found a use for toy airplanes with young burn patients: Children with burned hands could have fun twirling the propellers and get in some healing physical therapy, too. When toys broke, he fixed them.

Bill also made toys for the children of Southern Baptist medical workers and others on staff. But he was moved by the poverty of local children and families—and wanted to do something.

"It began with the toys, but it began to mushroom," says a close friend. "Bill's heart just began to be turned by these kids. They didn't have clothes. They didn't have school supplies. They didn't have drinking water. The more he saw, the bigger his heart became."

He tried for years to gain access to orphanages in the area and was denied. One day an important government official visited when Bill was in his woodworking shop. The official eyed a nearly completed toy truck on the worktable and finally asked if he could have it.

Sure, said Bill—if the official would help him get permission to visit the nearest orphanage. He had learned to do a little Yemeni-style bargaining after all.

The trade-off opened doors, and Bill began years of visiting orphans, bringing them toys, providing food, installing water pipes and plumbing, making sure they had medical care, even putting some through school. Many of Bill's toys were sold to raise money for needy kids.

"Going with Bill to the orphanage, it was always wonderful to see how those boys loved to see him come with that truck full of food and games," says a co-worker. "I remember one time he had bought all these bags of carrots. You would have thought it was $100 bills! The boys jumped on those carrots and were just gobbling them down. I thought to myself: What bunch of American kids would get excited about a bag of carrots?"

One boy Bill mentored and helped send to a university returned to teach at the orphanage where he grew up.

The ministry spread to widows with no family support, solitary divorced women, prison inmates, nomadic Bedouins—the poorest of the poor in a desperately poor region. Bill gave them wheat, sugar, tea, oil, beans, tomato paste.

He began funds for orphans and patients who couldn't pay their hospital bills. The funds continue to aid people to this day. When Bill was alive, much of the money came from the sale of his toys—or from his own pocket. No one knows how much.

Once, a worker tried to get an especially needy woman on Bill's "widows list." He said no.

"Why not?" the worker angrily demanded.

"Because I'm already giving her food," he said quietly. "Others need help more."

LAST DAYS

Evangelism was strictly forbidden in Islamic Yemen. Bill didn't consider himself much of an evangelist, anyway. But he loved people—all kinds of people in all walks of life. It made an impact even he didn't fully realize.

In recent years, one of Bill's grown orphan friends asked a younger worker for a Bible in Arabic. When Bill heard the good news later, he asked his colleague to close the office door.

"He just wept"—in joy and in sadness, says the worker. "He said, 'You've seen more in two years than I've seen in 25.' He was condemning himself as a missionary. But he had opened the doors with his ministry."

As the years passed and the demands increased, Bill struggled at times with exhaustion and nagging illnesses. For years he suffered excruciating pain when he walked from pins inserted in his hips after a car accident. Two hip replacements later eased the pain but didn't end it.

And always, there was the pressure to find more medical workers for the hospital.

"We are barely surviving now, and it will get worse," he wrote in early 2001 in an appeal for reinforcements. "Having only two doctors in the clinic will cause much anger as people come from other cities and are turned away … I have been recruiting for a long time and have not been successful. Do you have any ideas?"

> "HE JUST WEPT. HE SAID, 'YOU'VE SEEN MORE IN TWO YEARS THAN I'VE SEEN IN 25.' BUT HE HAD OPENED THE DOORS WITH HIS MINISTRY."

He lobbied hard for continued Southern Baptist administration of the hospital, however, even when the burdens became overwhelming.

When the transition to Yemeni government control began, there were "great differences of opinion about it," says the wife of a colleague who was firmly on the other side of the debate. "It was an emotional nightmare for both of them, but never did it affect their friendship or their deep respect for one another. Never was an unkind word said."

Her last memory of seeing Bill was at the annual Autumn Festival at Jibla in 2002. He quietly sat on a barrel, smiling as the hospital staff, local villagers, and children had fun.

"He was watching to make sure that we were all safe while the fair was being held," she remembers. "He was the leader, the shepherd, keeping watch over his flock."

In the days following the murders of Bill, Martha Myers and Kathy Gariety, deep grief swept through Jibla. Behind heavily guarded compound fences, hospital workers comforted one another. But villagers—many who had known and loved all three—had no one to turn to.

A few days after the shootings, Southern Baptist workers insisted on walking through the village after a memorial service—much to the dismay of security guards. They were swarmed by grieving Yemenis determined to express their respect and affection for the slain workers.

A man approached John Brady, International Mission Board regional leader for Northern Africa and the Middle East, and pulled out a little booklet of photos.

"THIS IS A MAN WHO TRULY LOVED US."

"He showed me a picture of a stool that Bill had worked on for the orphans," John recalls. "He showed me a picture of pipes Bill had bought and worked to get installed so the prisoners could have water. He showed me a picture of donkeys lined up with food on their backs to be carried out to widows and their families in the hills."

The villager closed the booklet and said, "This is a man who truly loved us."

Bill would have smiled. Then he probably would have said, "OK, folks, let's get back to work."

He was a workingman, after all. He came to this needy land, an admirer said, because a "sovereign God looked across the sea, had compassion for the people of Yemen—and chose someone to stand in the gap."

He chose a quiet grocer from Kansas.

KATHY GARIETY

obedient to the call

On a spring night in 1989, Keith Chase got a message from the Lord.

It came at the end of a Sunday evening service at Layton Avenue Baptist Church near Milwaukee, Wisconsin, where he was pastor. The Layton Avenue congregation was growing, but still counted fewer than a hundred members. The Sunday night crowd was even smaller.

But the divine message in Keith's mind was clear and specific: God was calling someone sitting in the pews to make a public commitment to foreign missions—that night, before anyone went home.

"In my many years of ministry, that kind of thing has happened only a handful of times—and I mean a handful," he stresses. "So I told the congregation, 'This is going to sound like I'm nuts, but I've got to be faithful to God. There's somebody here who is being called to foreign missions.'"

He had no clue who the person set apart by God might be. He wondered if it was one of the teens in the youth group, which comprised about a third of the church.

No one came forward. No one raised a hand.

In the awkward quiet, Pastor Keith sensed another divine impression: It was the last opportunity for this person to respond. Reluctantly but obediently, he relayed that message to the congregation, too—and waited.

Within seconds, Kathy Gariety stood up and walked down the aisle, tears streaming down her cheeks. Keith was dumbfounded. Kathy, age 39, wasn't a member of the youth group; she was the *minister* to youth—and a close friend of Keith and his wife. He knew she was a dedicated servant of the Lord, but the foreign mission call was a bombshell—to him and everyone else.

WITHIN SECONDS, KATHY GARIETY STOOD UP AND WALKED DOWN THE AISLE, TEARS STREAMING DOWN HER CHEEKS.

"She just bawled her eyes out," he remembers. "Come to find out she had received a call to foreign missions 12 years before and had put it off many times. She was crying out of guilt for not doing it before, but also out of joy for finally responding."

The decision may have been a long time coming, but once Kathy Gariety made it, there was no turning back. That's part of who she was.

Kathy was many things. A no-nonsense Midwesterner, with a strong dash of Irish stirred in. She was outspoken and quiet. Creative and practical. Artistic, yet highly organized. Frugal, yet generous. Strong, but tender. Independent—even ornery at times—yet loving and kind. Single throughout her adulthood, but deeply committed to family, friends, Christian community, the lost, and needy.

Most of all, she was obedient to Christ.

Kathleen Anne Gariety was born October 14, 1949, into an Irish Catholic family in Milwaukee. Her parents, Jerome and Mary Gariety, worked in local schools. He was a custodian; she was a parish teacher. They had little extra money to spend on Kathy, her older sister, Mary, or their younger siblings, Jerry and Patricia. But the family was close and the home was filled with love.

"Mother made sure we were in church," Jerry says. "But the simple little things she told us were what molded us, like, 'Treat each other as you would want to be treated.' When Christmas came around, we didn't always have a toy under the tree, but we were taught it was far better to give than to receive. The most important thing was sharing."

KATHY WAS MANY THINGS. ARTISTIC, YET HIGHLY ORGANIZED. STRONG, BUT TENDER. INDEPENDENT—EVEN ORNERY AT TIMES—YET LOVING AND KIND.

The Gariety kids loved winter ice skating in the back yard, baseball, Catholic youth activities. Sisters Kathy and Mary, a year apart in Catholic parochial schools, played on some championship volleyball teams for Mother of Good Counsel parish. Kathy discovered and began developing her artistic talents.

Early on, she also displayed serious interest in spiritual things—and in missions.

"During those years I met several missionaries," she wrote of the time. "Sister Therista was my homeroom teacher, and I frequently helped her box and wrap packages of clothing and books to be sent overseas. She told stories of the missionaries as we worked.

"On the eve of Mother's Day one year, I told my mother I wanted to be a missionary. In her wisdom, she said, 'That is the greatest gift a child could give her mother!' But she didn't push me to enter into the convent. We never again talked about it."

Some relatives wondered if Kathy would become a nun. Instead, she pursued her artistic gift, earning a degree in fine arts at the University of Wisconsin in Milwaukee. To make a living, she accepted a faculty position as textbook specialist at the campus bookstore where she had worked her way through college. She later became a bookstore manager at universities in Indiana, Illinois, and Michigan before returning to Wisconsin to manage several college bookstores in the Milwaukee area.

Those years gave her plenty of experience and expertise in business and handling inventory, which would prove invaluable later.

Her mother's death in 1971, when Kathy was a college senior, hit her hard. She began to question her faith and stopped going to church. In Michigan, however, a Christian boss she worked with challenged her to seek God anew.

"He awoke in me two questions that had haunted me earlier: 'Why do I believe in God?' and 'Who is God to me?'" Kathy reflected. "I knew all about Jesus and the Bible, but I didn't have peace. All my life I was taught that I was supposed to know, love, and serve the Lord with my whole heart, soul, and mind. But although I knew *about* Jesus, I did not know Him."

She met Jesus Christ personally in 1976, when she embraced Him as her Savior through the ministry of Packard Road Baptist Church in Ann Arbor, Michigan. She quickly became involved in youth work, loved it, and continued in youth ministry when she returned to Milwaukee two years later and joined Layton Avenue.

Kathy's ministry to youth was part time—but wholehearted. A parade of young people later testified to her impact on their lives during those years. Jenni Schwager related to Kathy almost daily from her first day of middle school through her senior year in high school.

> "WE DID SO MANY THINGS TOGETHER AS A YOUTH GROUP. I DON'T THINK I EVER HEARD HER SAY NO TO A REQUEST FROM ONE OF US —EVEN IF IT MEANT CRAMMING SIX OR SEVEN OF US INTO HER LITTLE RED FORD ESCORT TO GO AND HAVE PIE AFTER A SUNDAY EVENING SERVICE."

"We did so many things together as a youth group," Jenni remembers. "Summer camps, lock-ins, picnics. We went all over the place. Kathy was such a giving person. I don't think I ever heard her say no to a request from one of us—even if it meant cramming six or seven of us into her little red Ford Escort to go and have pie after a Sunday evening service. She became a mentor to me and to many others. Her life reflected the life of Christ through her constant servanthood."

UNCONDITIONAL SURRENDER

By the time Keith Chase came to Layton Avenue as pastor in 1987, Kathy had firm ideas about the way things should be done—in youth ministry and other areas of the church.

"We developed a deep respect for each other, but we butted heads fairly often in private," Keith acknowledges. "She had a very strong will; she was opinionated. But over time she began to see God blessing some of the things we were leading the church to do, and she changed her mind. It takes a mature person to do that."

Meanwhile, Kathy had been struggling for years with her inner sense of calling from the Lord.

"In 1980 I committed my life to full-time Christian service," she later wrote. "I began to think about my talk with my mother, but wasn't willing to commit myself to missions. I rationalized, 'Wisconsin is a mission area, so why should I go elsewhere when there's such a need right where I am?'"

She attended seminary classes when she could and became more and more involved in youth work, but "hid the call to foreign missions in my heart, continually trying to convince God I was doing missions."

The struggle came to an end when she surrendered to God's clear call on that Sunday evening in 1989. But another three years would pass before she went abroad. Her father, who was suffering from Alzheimer's disease, needed extensive assistance from the family. Kathy helped her sisters care for him.

Quietly, however, she began the missionary application process through the Foreign (now International) Mission Board. Pastor Keith, familiar with the mysteries of God's call, encouraged her however he could.

One day he heard a knock on his office door. Kathy walked in waving a document from the Foreign Mission Board. It listed more than a hundred possible missionary assignments and locations around the world.

"I'm not sure where to go," she confessed. "There are so many places I think I could be used."

"That may be so, but you need to ask God to make clear exactly where He wants you to be," he answered.

"OK, but how do I know?"

"You'll know."

"That doesn't help me at all!" she fumed, walking out. Keith smiled. Similar scenes continued for about six months, until the day of clarity arrived.

"I'll never forget it," he says. "She barged in—no knock, no nothing—and had this Cheshire-cat grin on her face, ear to ear. She said, 'Keith, I know!'

> "SHE BARGED IN—NO KNOCK, NO NOTHING —AND HAD THIS CHESHIRE-CAT GRIN ON HER FACE, EAR TO EAR. SHE SAID, 'I KNOW WHERE GOD IS CALLING ME!'"

'Know what?'

'I know where God is calling me!'"

It was Yemen, an ancient, isolated land on the Arabian Peninsula—with a Baptist hospital in urgent need of someone to manage supplies and purchasing.

"She had researched that opportunity as well as others," Keith says. "But with that one, God had touched her heart in a big way. She fell in love with the people, just looking at pictures. God said, 'This is it. This is where I want you.'"

Kathy was excited about going to the Middle East. Concerned family members weren't. They worried about her safety abroad—particularly in that volatile part of the world—and about how she would be treated as a single woman in one of the strictest Muslim societies in the region.

"We said, 'Go to Appalachia or something, not overseas,'" recalls Mary Quirk, an older cousin who was close to Kathy throughout her life. "But you answer the call where it comes from."

Knowing Kathy, they also knew deep down that no amount of persuasion would turn her back from following the voice she heard within.

Kathy's father died November 2, 1991. After helping care for him until his passing, she was ready for the next step of her life. Three months later she was appointed a Southern Baptist missionary. By the summer of 1992 she had arrived in Yemen—her home for the next decade.

Kathy experienced all the cultural shocks any new missionary faces—and then some.

Even by the Middle East's age-old standards, Yemen was tradition-bound. Yemeni Arabs adhered to a mixture of rigid Islam and ancient tribal customs. Far from the nation's few urban centers, 90-bed Jibla Baptist Hospital perched in the mountains that once were the fabled home of Solomon's Queen of Sheba. Poverty ruled in the countryside. Rural Yemeni women were seldom heard in public—and rarely seen behind their black veils.

For a single, independent-minded American woman like Kathy, Yemen was strong medicine.

"Yemen will drive you mad with frustration," says a male missionary who didn't have to deal personally—as Kathy did—with the culture's heavy restrictions on women. "I came home after my first term saying I wasn't going back. You've got to grow. Kathy was in that growing stage when I knew her."

She grew. She persevered. She stuck it out when civil war ravaged a divided Yemen during her early years in the country. She stuck it out when she had to deal with Yemeni merchants who refused—at first—to negotiate with her.

"It was hard for her as a woman to work in the position she had," says a female missionary who prayed with Kathy and watched her in action. "She had to deal with Yemeni men who had no respect whatsoever for women. When an Arab man will not even look at you or acknowledge your existence, just because you're a woman, it's hard.

"You overcome with a gentle and quiet spirit, doing the job and loving people as you go."

> "KATHY WAS ALL BUSINESS. THE HOSPITAL
> STORES WERE HER FIEFDOM, AND SHE
> RAN A TIGHT SHIP."

Not that Kathy lost her feistiness when it was needed—or her management skills. She found a hospital supply system in dire need of better organization and set about organizing it. She decreased waste and inefficiency. She carefully cultivated contacts with suppliers in many countries.

"Kathy was all business," reports a colleague who learned the supply operation from her when he arrived in Yemen. "She saved that hospital lots and lots of money just by being a good businesswoman. The hospital stores were her fiefdom, and she ran a tight ship."

Her reputation for locating things the hospital needed—and getting them delivered to isolated Jibla—eventually approached mythical heights. She found not just the essentials, but delightful extras to relieve the exhausting grind for workers who cared for hundreds of patients a day. Turkey on Thanksgiving for the hospital staff. Chickens (one of her favorite dishes) from France. Butter from Denmark. Assorted goodies for the hundreds of internationals who attended annual Christmas gatherings at her house.

Once, she conspired with her sister Mary back in Wisconsin to deliver a big package of marshmallows. Surprised hospital workers enjoyed roasting them over a bonfire on Christmas Eve.

Folks from Layton Avenue Baptist—and other churches she visited all over Wisconsin and the Midwest—became regular, enthusiastic links in Kathy's supply chain. Gathering materials for Jibla hospital became a year-round team effort. Kathy came home on periodic "foraging" trips to load up stuff to take back to Jibla.

"It could be anything from medical supplies to ceiling tiles to mattresses," says sister Mary, who helped coordinate supplies and handled Kathy's business affairs at home. "Once she took back 20 mattresses in a shipping container that was already so full they had to cram 'em in the back. I mean she would pack every inch.

"She bought some of it, but a lot of it was donated. She would go to Sam's Club or Wal-Mart and get cases and cases of paper towels and toilet paper. The hospital would be faxing to say, 'We need this type of wire or that part for the pickup truck.' She was always adding until the day she left. It was a never-ending list!"

One time Wal-Mart had a big sale on bed sheets. Kathy dispatched a church strike force to buy up every sheet at every Wal-Mart in greater Milwaukee.

Churchwomen bought flannel by the truckload and made thousands of baby blankets on sewing machines set up in the fellowship hall. The hospital used them to swaddle new arrivals; grateful Yemeni mothers took them home with their babies.

ONE TIME WAL-MART HAD A BIG SALE ON BED SHEETS. KATHY DISPATCHED A CHURCH STRIKE FORCE TO BUY UP EVERY SHEET AT EVERY WAL-MART IN GREATER MILWAUKEE.

"We had a blast trying to get everything we could find to send to Yemen," recalls Linda McKnight, who joined Layton Avenue the year Kathy was appointed a missionary. "It was so much fun to support her in any way we could. Just being around her was being around love."

It *was* fun—in a loading-Kathy's-Ark kind of way. Layton Avenue served as a storage warehouse at first. Later the church bought a nearby house with a garage where supplies could be stacked. The effort became a Christian witness to the community and the state. Secular businesses gladly got involved when they learned about the needs of struggling Yemenis and how the hospital met them.

"We would be the center for people to send us things all year," says Pastor Keith. "Hospitals would donate things. People would donate things. Every year Kathy would come home and pack one of these seagoing shipping containers. I think the next-to-last one we packed had somewhere in the neighborhood of $150,000 worth of useable supplies for the hospital, free and clear, just for the cost of shipping.

"Don't get me wrong. I love the Cooperative Program. It's one of the main reasons I'm Southern Baptist; we put our money where our mouth is when it comes to missions. But where people can become personally involved beyond financial giving, it's a big-time blessing. It became a rallying point, a celebration. People loved it."

Kathy was good at delivering the big stuff. And the little stuff. In Yemen, as in Wisconsin, she seemed to have a sixth sense about what people needed—whether they knew it or not. She would find it, or create it. She was an artist, after all.

"One of her greatest pleasures in life was making things and giving them away," remembers her cousin Mary. "She just had a generosity of spirit."

One morning worker Pam Brassert was in the stores area of the Jibla hospital compound, looking for eggs. She noticed some little Yemeni tea glasses on the shelf.

"Kathy, what are these here for?" she inquired.

"Oh, I don't know," Kathy mused. "I just thought somebody might want some and not have a chance to buy them in the market. So I thought I'd put some here. You can buy them if you want."

In that moment, Pam saw something behind Kathy's business-like exterior. She saw something the busy hospital workers didn't see every day, but it was always there.

"It was so thoughtful, so insightful," Pam says. "I got a glimpse into who Kathy really was."

Not everyone noticed who Kathy really was.

To find the real Kathy, you had to look beneath the bustle of purchasing and inventories, the bargaining with suppliers, the hard-nosed practicality. Those things were important. They came with her job, which she handled like the professional she was.

But they weren't Kathy.

Kathy's life passion revolved around relationships—with God, with others, and with helping others get closer to each other and to God. In many ways, large and small, the Jibla hospital community would not have been a real community without Kathy.

"KATHY WAS THE GLUE THAT HELD THE COMPOUND TOGETHER."

"Kathy was the glue that held the compound together," observes a nurse who spent three years working at Jibla.

"The thing about glue is you usually don't see it. She was the unseen hand that was responsible for coordinating all our holiday events. She made the Christmas, Thanksgiving, Autumn Fair, and Easter events that we—and internationals all over the country—looked forward to."

Kathy painted, decorated, arranged, did much of the footwork for such gatherings. They were more than a chance to take a break from work, enjoy a taste of home, or have a party. They helped turn the staff into a family—and the believers on staff into a Christian community.

The spiritual significance of that aspect of Kathy's ministry can hardly be overestimated. For decades, the little multipurpose room on the Jibla compound had been the only place in this strictly Muslim country where Christians could come together openly for worship and fellowship. Kathy helped make such times more frequent— and so much more meaningful.

At any given time, the Jibla Baptist Hospital counted 40 to 60 internationals on staff. Often only a half or a third of them were Southern Baptist medical workers, volunteers, or other American workers. Doctors and nurses came from around the world to work for months or years at a time. Wherever they came from, they all needed somebody who would try to make Jibla—if it couldn't *be* home—at least *feel* like home.

That was Kathy.

"She would spend time with the children of international workers teaching art classes," a co-worker explains. "She would reach out to volunteers to make their stay in Yemen something special. She would take the day off to drive volunteers several hours so they could say they had seen the Red Sea. That investment paid off again and again. During my stay in Yemen, many of the short-term volunteers became long-term partners there.

"Kathy strengthened, supported, and even helped expand the international Christian community. She helped foster the bonds of fellowship that sustained us through the joys and struggles of living in a dark land separated from our countries and families. Anyone who has lived overseas knows how immensely valuable that is."

The co-worker attended several memorial services for Kathy and her two slain colleagues, Bill Koehn and Martha Myers, in the days following the shootings. She was surprised to find that some of the international hospital workers knew Kathy—the "behind the scenes" member of the trio—better than they knew Bill or Martha.

The nature of their schedules accounted for some of it. "Mr. Bill" had the daunting daily task of overseeing the entire hospital operation. When "Dr. Martha" wasn't treating patients or performing surgery, she often headed into villages hither and yon to visit Yemenis where they lived. Kathy, meanwhile, focused closer to home.

She invited tired hospital staffers over for tea and sympathy. She cooked up a good meal for them. She took their kids into her heart, teaching Sunday School, coming up with fun arts-and-crafts projects. Once, she made papier-mâché Nativity scenes for every kid on the compound.

Kathy helped the hospital compound become a community. But she didn't have the "compound mentality" that sometimes isolates missionaries from the people they serve. Unlike most of the workers at Jibla, she didn't even live on the compound. Her home was a small house—within walking distance, but outside hospital walls—in the nearby village of Jibla.

"That's where she thought she belonged—among the people," says her cousin Mary. "She liked to be where they were, and she loved the children."

The children loved her, too.

Seldom did she go anywhere in the village without a ragtag band of Yemeni kids following her. Pastor Keith visited Jibla in 2001 and personally experienced her young "entourage."

One day during his visit, Keith and Kathy took a shortcut from the hospital to her house—an apparently deserted mountain path. It should have taken no more than five minutes to walk.

"The first thing we encountered was three kids playing some kind of game," Keith recounts. "They look up, yell 'Kathy!' and come running over and dive-bomb into her. One of them leaps up about two feet to grab her arms and legs and hug her. There was nobody around and all of a sudden they were everywhere—20 or more kids surrounding Kathy, just loving her and wanting to be with her."

Children loved the special things Kathy made for them. They loved it when she dressed up like a clown—a ministry she had begun back home in Wisconsin. She brought big smiles to the faces of kids in the hospital wards recovering from illness or surgery and screams of laughter to the halls of local orphanages.

When she first came to Jibla, trash on the streets bothered her. So she made a deal with local kids: Pick up a bag full of trash and deliver it to Kathy—and get a ball of your own to play with. It worked fine for a while, until word really got around.

"Kids were going all over the countryside raiding garbage cans to get trash to bring to Kathy for a ball," recalls her roommate, Ruth Anne McConnell. "We had tons of garbage coming to the house. She had to put a stop to that one."

But she found lots of other ways to help Yemenis—and be a friend to children, families, and women. She and Ruth Anne forged deep bonds with their landlord's family and others in the area.

"Kathy was very close to them," Ruth Anne says. "I think it was just a matter of being there, being available for people to drop in, stopping to chat with people as we walked up and down the road."

Kathy also gave quietly to Yemenis in need. She operated a clothes closet for the poor, gave food to hungry families, helped women with emergency aid, visited orphans.

"She wanted to have every opportunity for the people to see her living with them, eating their food, getting to know them," explains

Keith. "She wanted to use these relationships to bring Christ into their lives. That was her goal before she even got on the field.

"That's who she was."

"... UNTIL GOD TELLS ME TO GO HOME"

Kathy experienced some difficult times in her last year at Jibla. She made no secret of her opposition to the International Mission Board's decision to turn the hospital over to the Yemeni government.

On a wider scale, threats against Americans in Yemen and the Arab world increased, creating new tensions for missionaries and other foreign workers at the hospital. The September 11, 2001, attacks against the United States increased those tensions. A number of international staffers left Jibla and went home in the days and months after 9/11. Kathy's family urged her to do the same.

"We became adamant about trying to get her to come home," says her brother, Jerry.

Kathy responded to relatives' and friends' concerns by downplaying any dangers. Media reports were blowing things out of proportion, she insisted. Either way, she had no intention of leaving.

"I firmly believe that I have been called to Yemen, specifically to Yemen," she told a visitor. "If I hadn't been called to Yemen, I probably would have been gone already, because there have been some times when you think, 'It's not worth it. Let's go home.' But then I'm reminded of how strong my calling was to come, and I think there's a reason for being here.

"I might not know what one little thing it is that I'm here to do, but I'm here, and I will continue to stay here until God tells me to go home."

God called her home—into His arms—on the morning of December 30, 2002, as she sat in an office on the hospital compound with her long-time colleagues Bill Koehn and Martha Myers.

In the moment just before they were fatally shot, what went through Kathy's mind? Keith Chase believes she saw Jesus standing to welcome her, Bill, and Martha—as he welcomed Stephen, the first

I FIRMLY BELIEVE THAT I HAVE BEEN CALLED TO YEMEN, SPECIFICALLY TO YEMEN. I MIGHT NOT KNOW WHAT ONE LITTLE THING IT IS THAT I'M HERE TO DO, BUT I'M HERE, AND I WILL CONTINUE TO STAY HERE UNTIL GOD TELLS ME TO GO HOME."

Christian martyr. He believes she heard the Lord say, "Well done, good and faithful servant."

He also believes—with all his heart—that she prayed for the salvation of her killer.

What "one little thing," as she called it, was Kathy Gariety sent to Yemen to do?

There were thousands of things, of course. Many were never seen by anyone other than Christ—and won't be known until He reveals all things one day.

A recent encounter, however, can stand for many of Kathy's acts of love.

A worker who was trained by Kathy when he first came to Yemen, continues to minister in the nation. One day he and his wife befriended a young widow who became a believer. The young woman went home and led her brother to believe. They returned to visit her new friends and invited them to visit their home in an extremely poor village area.

As they drank tea, the young woman asked, "Did you know Miss Kathy?"

The visitors replied that they had known her well.

"Oh!" the woman cried. "She's been here many times."

Kathy laid the groundwork for so much through her many quiet relationships. "One of our doctors once said, 'If it takes 10 genuine attempts at sharing before a person listens, are you willing to be the ninth one every time?' " the worker says. "I think Kathy often was. I've been in many houses where people have said, 'Kathy Gariety used to come and visit us.' "

Back home, folks will never forget Kathy. They cried at her memorial service at Layton Avenue, but they also celebrated.

"She was a consistent presence in my life for 14 years," testified Clara Alcott, a young woman who grew up in Kathy's youth group. "At first, I didn't understand why she would want to go to Yemen. But she understood that God doesn't have boundaries in His heart. He doesn't have country lines. He doesn't see people that way. Kathy was like that, too. She was where God wanted her to be. She was where she wanted to be. I can only grieve to a certain point because I know God's will has been done.

"Kathy is still my teacher. I saw somebody finish the race sprinting."

Kathy still teaches a lot of people—especially young people.

On the day she died, a missionary couple who had gone through appointment and training with Kathy a decade before, watched the television news reports of the shootings and cried together. They had been going through some boxes of mementos from the attic that day, and their youngest daughter came across a yellowing piece of paper in her "memory box" marked with the words "Happy Gram."

"IF IT TAKES TEN GENUINE ATTEMPTS AT SHARING BEFORE A PERSON LISTENS, ARE YOU WILLING TO BE THE NINTH ONE EVERY TIME? I THINK KATHY OFTEN WAS."

The note contained a Bible verse, Isaiah 40:29: "He giveth power to the faint; and to them that have no might He increaseth strength."

A short prayer at the end of the note read: "Dear Jesus, help me to walk in the courage of my faith."

"Mom, turn over the paper and read the other side," the daughter said. These words were on the back: "From Kathy Gariety at the Missionary Learning Center, May 1992."

"God allowed us to find it on the day of her death," the missionary says. "This small note, written to encourage a child 10 years before, was now a testimony of God's power for the faint and His strength for those who have no might."

Her life still speaks to the people she loved in Yemen—and to us.

MARTHA MYERS

'things don't matter, people do.'

3

To see Martha Myers, M.D., for what ailed you, you had to get in line.

No surprise there. Most of us know what it's like waiting in exam rooms for doctors. The difference with "Dr. Martha": Once she got around to you, you were the most important person on the planet.

With her gentle expression and toothy smile, she seemed to have all the time in the world to heal your hurt, to talk, maybe just to listen. Kind of like Jesus with the multitudes.

What's more, she made house calls—even if she had to wake you up in the middle of the night to get into your house.

Martha's philosophy: "Things don't matter, people do."

"Things" included not only possessions and position, but rules, plans, timetables. It drove her busy co-workers crazy sometimes, since so many other patients needed to be seen. But that's the way she was, whether you encountered her at the hospital, on the street—or 10 miles off the last identifiable road, where some of her best Yemeni friends lived.

In fact, much of craggy, mountainous Ibb Province in the Middle Eastern land of Yemen was Dr. Martha's waiting room. Men, women, and children gathered before dawn to see her at the Jibla Baptist Hospital, one of the few full-service medical facilities in the impoverished Arab country of 19 million people. When she drove into their mountain villages or parked by the side of rocky roads to hold health clinics, people lined up for hours.

"EVERYBODY KNEW HER, AND SHE KNEW EVERYBODY."

Sometimes families just camped beside the door to her apartment, up the hill from the hospital. They figured she had to come home to sleep sooner or later.

"Everybody knew her, and she knew everybody," says a hospital worker.

That included not only the poor country folk of Ibb but high-powered sheiks, government officials and urban residents who trekked to Jibla for the kind of medical care Martha became renowned for.

It was worth the trip—and worth the wait.

"Martha Myers loved the people of Yemen—and they knew it," recalls a friend who worked alongside her. "She took her time with each patient in the clinic. If you remember that Jibla hospital saw 40,000 patients a year, that statement takes on more weight. On her 'days off,' she would load her Land Rover with medical supplies and drive over rough roads to reach out-of-the-way villages, where she would be welcomed as a dear friend."

Even the man who killed her had to wait.

Abed Abdul Razak Kamel patiently sat in the open-air courtyard of the hospital on the morning of December 30, 2002, clutching an outpatient clinic "ticket" for a follow-up medical consultation.

When Martha hurried through, he followed her into hospital administrator Bill Koehn's office and methodically shot her, Bill, and supply manager Kathy Gariety.

His grievance? Martha and her hospital colleagues apparently loved Yemenis too much—including Kamel's wife, whom Martha had treated and befriended.

The Christian doctor's compassion reportedly enraged Kamel, who had ties to a Muslim extremist group. He claimed Martha and other medical workers were trying to convert Muslims to Christianity, which is forbidden in the conservative Islamic nation. By killing them, he said, he was "getting closer to God."

Too bad Kamel didn't get to know Martha. Seeing her in action might have helped him get closer to God, if that's what he really desired.

Some admirers dubbed her "the Baptist Mother Teresa" in the flood of tributes that followed her death. If she were still here, Martha surely would reject that description. So would some of the colleagues who loved her most—and butted heads with her regularly.

"She could be *so* exasperating!" sighs one long-time co-worker.

For those who think missionaries are "saints" rather than forgiven sinners—and therefore most of us aren't cut out for missions—let's establish something up front: Martha was quite human. She had her share of foibles and more than her share of quirks.

She was totally, resolutely her own person, for better or worse. Having shed Western concepts of time long ago, she came and went on her own "schedule" and lived in her own world. She seldom slept at her apartment, which was essentially a storehouse packed with stuff she collected or bought to give away to needy Yemenis.

She didn't sleep much at all, for that matter; "night person" is an understatement in Martha's case. She loved animals, including snakes and scavengers, which delighted her many "missionary kid" buddies—and horrified their mothers whenever a grinning Martha arrived with some creature on her arm.

"Dr. Martha was, well, Dr. Martha," says one admirer. "Many people said she had a gift for seeing 'outside the box.' I'm not sure she knew where the box was."

She disappeared into the Yemeni countryside for days at a time, visiting friends and families. She caused near-mutinies among the

> "WE COULD NOT MEET EVERY NEED THAT WAS PRESENTED TO US; IT WAS JUST IMPOSSIBLE. BUT MARTHA DIDN'T BELIEVE THAT."

hospital staff on occasion—particularly when she performed elective surgeries after midnight, or insisted on seeing clinic patients at 5 p.m. when the clinic was supposed to close at 2.

Once, she hid a late-arriving burn patient in an operating room so he couldn't be transferred to another hospital. She was determined the patient would get the kind of care only Jibla could give, regardless of the rules. Hospital staffers were not amused.

"Her inability to follow guidelines was really frustrating, but it came out of her compassion," admits a hospital veteran who had multiple run-ins with Martha. "We could not meet every need that was presented to us; it was just impossible. But Martha didn't believe that."

She wasn't a "saint." But she did share a daily approach to life with Mother Teresa.

"Love until it hurts," the legendary missionary nun often challenged anyone who would listen. "We can only love God at our own expense."

Martha Myers loved God—and others—until it hurt. She gave everything she had to the people of Yemen—her time, her considerable medical gifts, her possessions, herself.

And, in the end, her life.

INSATIABLE COMPASSION

From childhood on, Martha always "had an insatiable compassion for people, especially people in need," observes Ira Myers, her father and mentor. The elder Myers is a distinguished physician in his own right and former public health director for the state of Alabama.

He won't take credit for it, but his daughter inherited some of her compassion from him—along with her love of medicine.

"I grew up in Birmingham, Alabama, until Daddy went to Seattle, Washington, for his medical internship," wrote Martha, who was born March 13, 1945. Early on, she and her younger brothers also experienced life in West Virginia, upstate New York and Massachusetts.

Their parents moved from place to place as Myers worked with the U.S. Public Health Service and later pursued advanced public health studies at Harvard. At each location, Ira and Dorothy Myers found a church where the family could worship—and the kids found places to run and play with animals.

"I finished first grade in Buffalo, New York," Martha recalled of the time. "We lived in an apartment directly across the street from a field ideal for running with our Samoyed dogs, hunting birds' nests and frightening ourselves by flushing pheasants."

In Boston, "the pond in the woods behind our house had a steep hill for sledding, and all winter long the big kids would go through our yard with ice skates over their shoulders. The setting was perfect for meeting salamanders, tadpoles, and snakes. Daddy tried to introduce us to the anatomy of an etherized frog, but I couldn't see the anatomy for the tears."

Even in places where other believers were hard to find, the Mycrses trained their children to love the Lord, told them "Wild West" stories from the Old Testament, rewarded them for memorizing Bible verses at bedtime.

Her father remembers Martha as a smart, alert, happy kid—always ready for action, always learning something new.

"Martha was a free spirit," he reflects. "But we never made a trip anywhere in the car that she didn't have at least two books with her, plus a notebook. She was an avid note taker. And she was always involved in everything church-related and God-related."

Young Martha didn't go on many medical calls with her dad, but she watched and absorbed his comings and goings in the service of humanity.

"I'm sure she learned some things from living in our house," Myers admits. "We were in public health service and I was on call 365 days a year to do whatever was needed."

Later he took the family back south, where he worked at the Center for Disease Control headquarters in Atlanta—interacting with colleagues like Jonas Salk, pioneer of the polio vaccine. They returned to Alabama in 1955, and Myers eventually became the state's chief health officer, a post he held for 32 years.

"Martha knew that any commitment to the field of medicine was going to take most of your time," Myers says. "But at the same time, I hope she learned that no matter what your responsibilities are in your job, you never forget your responsibilities to the Lord are your first and foremost obligation."

> "MY FRIEND LINDA OTT AND I PLANNED TO QUIT SCHOOL AS SOON AS THE LAW ALLOWED AND GO TO CHINA. MEANWHILE, THE CLASS BULLIES WERE OUR EVANGELISTIC TARGETS."

She learned. Her childhood church activity became soul-saving spiritual commitment during the showing of a Billy Graham evangelistic movie at church. Martha, age 8, went forward in tears after the film and was baptized soon after.

"Fourth grade was busy with Brownies, piano, choir, and GAs (Girls Auxiliary, now called Girls in Action, a missions education program for girls)," Martha recalled. "My friend Linda Ott and I planned to quit school as soon as the law allowed and go to China. Meanwhile, the class bullies were our evangelistic targets."

She zipped through school with top grades, stayed busy with music and other interests, and helped her mother raise baby sister Joanna Lynn—a new addition to the Myers family. But in the background, she said, "I was continually aware of a call to foreign missions, and at 12 I consciously realized that medicine could provide a satisfying and effective life for sharing Christ's love."

It was her realization—and her own decision.

"I learned about her decision to go into medicine secondhand," her father says. "She made up her own mind. That was between her and the Lord."

Martha finished her undergraduate work at Samford University in Birmingham and studied medicine at the Medical College of Alabama (University of Alabama) in Birmingham—her father's alma mater.

While still a medical student, she first visited Yemen for two months in 1971 as a short-term worker with the Southern Baptist Foreign (now International) Mission Board.

"When she told me she was going to Yemen, I said, 'Well, where is that?'" her father recalls with a chuckle. "I'd heard of it, but I didn't know where it was."

In this ancient land where the Queen of Sheba once ruled, Martha experienced life at the young Jibla Baptist Hospital—and the staggering needs it was trying to meet. At the time, Yemen counted one doctor for every 160,000 people. The infant-to-age-5 mortality rate reached as high as 50 percent.

Yemen was heavily influenced by age-old tribal traditions and conflicts—and still ruled in some areas by sheiks and warlords. More modern regional and political struggles would later cause civil war. All in all, went the cliché, Yemen was "rushing headlong into the fifteenth century."

Martha encountered people who had never laid eyes on a doctor, much less been treated by one. Desperately ill Muslim women who could not be examined by male doctors because of social strictures. Mothers dying needlessly in childbirth. Children dying of hunger and preventable diseases.

But the young med student was captivated. Here was a place that needed all the skill—and love—she could ever hope to give.

"I was touched by the Yemeni," she later wrote with simple understatement. The experience would change her life forever.

When Martha returned home, she informed her parents God was leading her toward long-term service in Yemen. "This is where the Lord has called me to go," she declared. "I'm going to do everything I can from this point on to prepare myself."

"Well, what all did you see?" her father asked.

"You wouldn't believe it!" she replied. She described some of her most vivid cases, such as assisting in a critical post-cranial operation —brain surgery on someone with a crushed skull, in other words.

"They just need hands. They need help," she said. "It's where I'm needed."

> "THEY JUST NEED HANDS. THEY NEED HELP. IT'S WHERE I'M NEEDED."

That was it. There was no discussion of lost potential income— or lost opportunities for a prestigious U.S. medical career. Martha wasn't interested in medicine for its own sake, in the first place. She never lost sight of God's call to her as a 12-year-old. Medicine was to be her tool for sharing the love of Christ. She may have been a free spirit, but she had remarkable "stickability" on key issues, according to her father.

Marriage? "I felt a special assurance from the Lord that Yemen was where I would be and, single or not, I would be happy," she said.

Martha completed her internship and residency at the University of South Alabama Medical Center in Mobile. She spent that time and her first few years of private practice focusing on obstetrics, gynecology, and general surgery—the skills she would need most at

> "I FELT A SPECIAL ASSURANCE FROM THE LORD THAT YEMEN WAS WHERE I WOULD BE AND, SINGLE OR NOT, I WOULD BE HAPPY."

Jibla. She also concentrated on growing spiritually through the ministry of Dauphin Way Baptist Church in Mobile.

She returned to Yemen as a career missionary doctor after her appointment by the Foreign Mission Board in 1977 and began fulfilling the purpose for which she was born.

TOTAL IMMERSION

Missionaries often talk about cultural immersion—the sponge-like process of absorbing and understanding the language, culture, customs, folkways, and values of the people you seek to serve. It takes a lifetime, but needs to start on day one if you want to make a real impact where God places you.

In Martha's case, the immersion was near-total. She remained an American, a Southerner, above all a bold and vital Christian. Unlike many workers who struggle for years with cultural adjustment, however, she enthusiastically jumped off a high cliff into the strange new ocean of Yemeni life.

It started with Arabic, which she studied with characteristic intensity before starting at Jibla. Within a few years she was speaking and listening like a native—not just the words, but the idioms, the nuances, the hidden meanings that reveal the hearts and minds of people.

"Most of her closest friends were Yemeni, and she spoke the language like a Yemeni," observes an American co-worker. "She *was* a Yemeni. You could just watch her walking with a Yemeni friend. She'd have her straw hat on, and she would throw back her head and laugh over something the rest of us didn't understand. She understood Yemeni humor. They tell jokes in Arabic and even though we speak Arabic, we don't get it. She got it!"

She talked like a Yemeni, ate like a Yemeni, dressed like a Yemeni—minus the veil that covers many Muslim women. That wholehearted commitment—coupled with her compassion and medical skills—won her countless Yemeni friends. And once you have an Arab friend, you have a friend for life.

"Martha *was* the hospital."

"Martha *was* the hospital," observes a colleague. "The Yemenis loved her. After she saw them they might give her a little gift—old used beads, a cracked vase, some grapes, or a bag of dried fish."

It was all they had. It was plenty for Martha.

In the hospital wards, on the streets of Ibb and Jibla, in the villages, the chorus was the same whenever she was spotted: "Ya Doctora! Doctora Martha!"

Even long-time hospital manager Bill Koehn, no stranger to endless demands for his attention, marveled at the phenomenon.

"Half the world is looking for you, Martha!" he once told her.

Part of it was the crushing patient load. Jibla Baptist Hospital, which eventually grew to 90 beds, treated thousands of patients a month and handled hundreds of surgeries. Southern Baptist doctor James Young founded the hospital in the 1960s, and it was owned and operated by the International Mission Board until the end of 2003. To cope with the onslaught of needs, however, it depended on short-termers and medical contract workers from many countries in addition to career Southern Baptist medical workers like Myers.

"It's a continual struggle," she acknowledged in the mid-1990s. "The turnover is very high and very stressful. You go from feast to famine. You may have 13 doctors one month and feel like you're pretty well-staffed, then another month you're down to two—and don't know how you're going to survive."

For Martha, patient rounds and surgeries often turned into round-the-clock marathons fueled by her one material indulgence: Coca-Cola. Once, when the hospital was full, she turned her own living room into a temporary ward.

"She went from event to event," says one co-worker. "She could exhaust you in a day—and drive you crazy in a week."

Martha often grabbed a few hours of sleep on the floor under her desk, in the hospital library—or on a mat beside a feverish infant's crib. She ate meals where she found them, which was pretty easy considering the Arab world's culture of hospitality and her legions of friends.

"She had an open-door policy," a friend explains. "If your door was open, she would come in for dinner, or maybe breakfast if she had worked all night." She'd eat and head back to work, perhaps stuffing some cold pancakes into her pocket to snack on later.

Bed and breakfast (or dinner) walk-ins were routine, too, and usually welcomed by folks who understood Martha's routine.

> "SHE HAD AN OPEN-DOOR POLICY. IF YOUR DOOR WAS OPEN, SHE WOULD COME IN FOR DINNER, OR MAYBE BREAKFAST IF SHE HAD WORKED ALL NIGHT."

"At night everything would be real quiet, and then we'd hear this tap-tapping at our door," remembers a Southern Baptist worker who lived on the hospital compound. "We'd go to the door and Martha would say, 'I've been working and it's too late to go home. Can I sleep on your sofa?' Then she'd say, 'Whatcha got in the refrigerator?' We didn't mind. It was fun."

GOOD MEDICINE, UNCONDITIONAL LOVE

Martha put her training in obstetrics/gynecology and surgery to good use in Yemen. For years she was one of only two Western-trained OB-GYNs in the whole country. Even today, infant mortality in Yemen runs at 66 per 1,000 live births—10 times the U.S. rate. One in 13 Yemeni women still die during childbirth. Many women receive no medical care at all, even if they live near a hospital or clinic, because of prohibitions against a male doctor touching female patients.

During her quarter-century at Jibla, Martha learned to practice nearly every type of medicine—and pioneered some new types, particularly when it came to caring for women and mothers.

A Southern Baptist physician remembers being taken under Martha's wing after experiencing "medical culture shock" when he confronted the needs at Jibla. She taught him how to cope—and overcome.

"Martha was a good surgeon," he says. "With limited resources she was able to do a lot of things. She learned how to improvise, how to do things a lot of people wouldn't think to do."

Example: Yemeni women frequently develop urinary infections and incontinence after bearing many children. In addition to the physical discomfort, they suffer the social stigma of being "unclean" in Yemen's conservative society. Martha worked hard to develop a simple surgical procedure to help solve the problem. Many women came long distances to seek relief.

"IT NEVER CEASED TO AMAZE ME THAT MARTHA COULD PRACTICE MEDICINE ANYWHERE."

What really impressed the young physician, however: Martha could diagnose patients anytime, anyplace.

"It never ceased to amaze me that Martha could practice medicine anywhere," he says. "We would be with her somewhere and someone would recognize her and come up and start telling her about their complaint. She would examine and diagnose, and if she didn't have the medicine in her Land Rover, she would go get it or buy it herself. Martha was a true 24/7 doctor."

How do you properly diagnose an illness on a city street corner —or on the side of a mountain road?

Practice.

"She'd lived there for 20 years, so she knew what diseases they got or if they had an amoeba or malaria," says another doctor who watched Martha in action. "I was just off the boat and just out of (medical) residency and I was saying, 'You just poked their stomach and you know they've got malaria?' I was shocked. How could she possibly know what's wrong with them? But you've got to go by what is the most likely problem and treat it, then if that doesn't work, go to the next most likely thing."

Many rural Yemenis, Martha well knew, could never get from their isolated homes to the hospital—and wouldn't be able to afford treatment if they did. So she treated them on the spot.

Once she treated a gunshot victim who needed a ventilator, which the Jibla hospital lacked. She took a newly arrived Southern Baptist doctor with her and searched the area until she found a government hospital with a ventilator.

"So we went back to Jibla and loaded him in the back of her Land Cruiser with his chest tubes and one of these great big oxygen tanks," the younger doctor says. "It was the patient, the oxygen tank, four other members of the patient's family, Martha, and me in the Cruiser. That was nothing for Martha. But she didn't have to do it; she went above and beyond. She was giving them what they needed, because she loved them."

Whether she was in the hospital or on the streets, Martha treated people with love. Even the dying would muster a smile when she spent time with them. That's something else Martha had in common with Mother Teresa.

Once she appeared at a new Southern Baptist worker's door on the compound. She urged the worker to come to one of the hospital wards—and to bring her 3-year-old daughter with her. A woman from a far-off village was dying in the ward, and no one was with her.

"We went and drew pictures for this lady, and we sang the one song we knew in Arabic," the worker remembers. "This woman was dying, but God turned it around, and she eventually was able to go home. She just needed a different touch, and Martha had the insight to know that."

Another time, Martha called the same worker and asked her to come and pray for a girl displaying all the signs of demonic possession. Other hospital staffers wrote it off as a psychological problem, but Martha saw a spiritual attack behind it. The family of the girl later told hospital workers they lived near someone who had put a curse on the girl, and that ever since, "Our house has been sick."

During one marathon day in the hospital, a colleague brought some cookies to an exam room so Martha could have something to eat during another long day. He walked in to find her gazing intently into the eyes of a young man lying on the table. His face had a sickly greenish hue; his eyes swam with agony.

"She was just holding his hand and staring into his eyes," the worker explains. "She wasn't saying a word, and he was staring back up at her. She didn't even know I was there."

The worker quietly slipped the cookies into Martha's lab coat pocket and backed out of the room. He later discovered the young man had attempted suicide by drinking insecticide. Martha had pumped his stomach but wanted to keep him in the hospital for observation. His family, however, wanted him released against medical advice.

"He was OK physically, but Martha wanted to make sure he was

OK emotionally. You don't talk to do that; you just look into their eyes. That's the kind of doctor she was."

The young man later became a believer.

IN THE VILLAGES

A typical day for Martha Myers?

"No day is typical," she answered during a 1994 interview. "Over the last two months we've dealt with a malaria epidemic, a diphtheria epidemic and a measles epidemic, while trying to do routine vaccinations and outreach at the same time."

In cooperation with UNICEF and the World Health Organization, she also started the hospital's mobile clinic and vaccination/immunization programs. The immunization program eventually extended into hundreds of villages in southern Yemen and saved thousands of lives—especially the lives of children.

It made her dad—a lifelong public health advocate—happy, too. "I told her, 'Congratulations, Martha. You're gonna save a lot more lives that way than you would just doing surgery and delivering babies,'" he recounts.

It also gave her a reason to get out into the countryside. Like the vanishing breed of small-town doctors in America, Martha obsessively focused on the births, lives, and deaths of whole communities —communities that were unseen and unknown to most.

As she drove her Land Rover through the mountains, back roads and dry wadis, people would appear—seemingly out of nowhere—crying "Doctora Martha!"

"The villagers would hear her vehicle coming and start walking out," says a doctor who often accompanied Martha. "You can't even see where they live when you drive up; they have to walk you up to their houses. She would have boxes of bread for them, and she would start holding a clinic right there in the back of the Cruiser, doing examinations and writing prescriptions. I think that's what she loved more than anything."

Another helper Martha recruited for trips got scared on one excursion when villagers surrounded the Land Rover and pressed in. It was time to go, but they wouldn't move.

"They were four and five deep around us, and we couldn't move the Cruiser," he recounts. "They wouldn't let her go. I was as nervous as a cat. But she just gently cranked up the car and eased off. It didn't bother her in the least."

> "THEY WERE FOUR AND FIVE DEEP AROUND US, AND WE COULDN'T MOVE THE CRUISER. THEY WOULDN'T LET HER GO. I WAS AS NERVOUS AS A CAT. BUT SHE JUST GENTLY CRANKED UP THE CAR AND EASED OFF. IT DIDN'T BOTHER HER IN THE LEAST."

If Martha promised a personal visit or a house call, it might take awhile, but she'd come. On her excursions, she frequently started out for one village but got diverted to another when she encountered a request for help. Eight, 10, 12 hours later, she would insist on continuing to her original destination.

"That was no problem to her," explains a co-worker. "She would just get to the village and toss a rock at a window to wake them. I remember saying, 'Martha! It's 3 o'clock in the morning. Let them sleep.' But she just kept throwing rocks and saying, 'No, no, no. I said I was going to visit, and that's what I'm going to do.'"

She loved to take workers and visitors at the hospital with her on excursions, often with no advance notice.

"The way I got to know Dr. Martha was by walking home from work, and she would ask, 'Are you coming off (shift) or going on?' " recalls a Southern Baptist nurse. "If I was coming off, she would inevitably say, 'Come with us; we have room for one more.' It took me a couple of immunization trips to realize that with Dr. Martha, no matter how full her Land Cruiser was, there was always room for 'one more.' "

Her favorite travel mates: missionary kids living on the hospital compound. The younger, the better. They enjoyed the adventure of a trip—and learned how to help out. One mother who nervously turned her children over to Martha from time to time found that she could be trusted to bring them back in one piece.

"My kids learned the first few times that if Mom says no, Aunt Martha says, 'Let's go!'" she explains with a rueful laugh. "But she adored our children. Other people on the compound would say, 'Do you realize you have just let your children go off with Martha, and they may not come home for days?' Then they would calm down and say, 'Well, somebody needs to have a regulating effect on Martha.' The kids would let her know when it was time to head back."

On most of Martha's journeys, the road would inevitably disappear and the wadis were the only routes to a destination. The Land Rover would start jolting up and down. As passengers bounced between the seats and the roof of the vehicle, Martha would grin mischievously into the rearview mirror and announce, "That'll be 25 cents for the ride."

Her father visited Yemen in later years and accompanied her on several such journeys. After experiencing one of her post-midnight home visits, when the host family insisted on entertaining their honored guests for half the night, he wearily asked, "You don't do this all the time, do you?"

"Oh, this is routine," she replied. "This is when you can do your best work, because nobody's watching."

"Martha, you've got more brass than a doorknob," said Dr. Myers, smiling and shaking his head.

Perhaps Martha's greatest daily struggle was feeling torn by the sheer number of needs. She couldn't treat everyone, help everyone, love everyone. If she stayed at the hospital, people in the villages went without care. If she stayed in the villages, people in the hospital suffered. And that was only the medical part of the equation; Martha wanted to focus on relationships.

"One of the hardest things is not having time to complete the work and continue relationships," she said in 1994. "Last week a friend of mine died, and I haven't been to see his wife. You have the same thing in the hospital, where you'd like to sit and talk to a patient but there are 10 others with urgent needs. Sometimes I think we come across as very uncaring."

Every death at the hospital hurt the medical workers who labored to save lives. They hurt Martha in ways no one else could fathom. The child who died because he was brought to Jibla one day too late. The mother who died after hours of futile surgery, leaving behind nine children. Each took its toll on Martha's heart.

Once, after a dispute with a Yemeni hospital worker during a stressful time, she vented her anger to a co-worker. Then without warning she asked, "Am I losing my compassion?"

"Here was the most compassionate person I ever knew, asking this question," the co-worker reflects. "I think she examined herself pretty regularly."

Her father understood Martha's struggle. He once reminded her, "Martha, you can't take care of everybody."

"I know," she sighed. "All I can do is what I can, when I can. The rest doesn't matter." But that didn't stop her from trying to do it all.

ETERNITY WILL TELL

Martha knew the risks of working in a place like Yemen, particularly as Islamic radicalism increased in recent years. She was carjacked and briefly held by Muslim militants in 1996. They forced her under a cover in the back of her Land Rover and drove it around the Yemeni countryside. When they threatened to kill her, she told them, "Well, I'll be in heaven."

The vehicle eventually ran out of gas and her captors fled when some villagers grew suspicious. Martha later downplayed the terror of the incident; kidnappings of foreigners for ransom was relatively common in some parts of Yemen. But it affected her in deeper ways.

"I think, in a sense, it broke her heart," says a friend. It may have been common for foreigners, "but she felt she was one of them. 'How could you treat me like a foreigner?' I think that was devastating for her."

Missionaries in particular, by the very nature of their service to local people and communities, are vulnerable. They don't work behind reinforced walls or travel in armed convoys. In the aftermath of Martha's killing, some voices criticized American missionary presence anywhere abroad, suggesting in particular that there's no good reason for medical professionals to put themselves in such peril.

Tell that to the thousands of people whose lives were saved,

WHEN THEY THREATENED TO KILL HER, SHE TOLD THEM, "WELL, I'LL BE IN HEAVEN."

whose babies were delivered, whose suffering was relieved by Martha. Tell it to the thousands who crowded around the hospital gates for days after the shootings, who lined the streets of Jibla for half a mile, who cried for the loss of their friend.

Years ago, Martha asked to be buried in Jibla if she died there. The request was honored by her family and her Yemeni friends, who built a casket and laid her to rest on the hospital's grounds the day after she died.

"Over here (in the United States), it would just be another grave," Martha's father said many times in the days after her death. "There, it's a testimony."

For her own part, Martha once said, "No prayers are wasted on Yemen, because the needs are so great. The fields are white unto harvest, and we need to pray to the Lord of the harvest to send out folks to help.

"I think the presence of the hospital is making an impact. Only eternity will really know what the impact is."

And one day, eternity will tell.

YEMEN AFTERWORD

For a time after the shootings, despair enveloped the hospital.

Hospital workers, stunned and weeping, comforted each other inside the compound, which was closed and heavily guarded after the killings. After the initial hours of caring for the dying and wounded had subsided, surgeon Judy Williams encountered a Yemeni co-worker who was a friend of Kathy's.

"WHY ARE YOU CRYING? THEY ARE NOT HERE! THEY ARE NOT IN THE GROUND. THEY ARE UP IN HEAVEN."

"I'm so sorry," he said, again and again, through his tears. "I'm so sad." All she could think to say to ease his pain was, "I understand."

The international workers gathered to remember their slain colleagues a few days later in Yemen's capital, Sanaa, where they were taken as officials evaluated the security situation in Jibla.

Many local Yemenis who loved Bill, Martha, and Kathy, however, had no one to turn to in their grief. The day after the attack, hundreds gathered outside the fence to watch as Bill and Martha were buried atop a hill on the hospital compound (Kathy's body was returned to her family in the United States for burial). Hundreds more lined the road for half a mile beyond the hospital gate.

The simple funeral was the first Christian burial—or Christian service of any kind—most of the people present that day had ever witnessed. Bill and Martha both considered Jibla their home; they had asked to be buried there if they died in Yemen. Yemenis at the hospital built simple caskets for the two—and dug the grave into which they were laid side by side. "He is Lord" was sung in Arabic; the Lord's Prayer was recited.

"The Yemenis just lined the fence," says a mourner who stood on the hill that day. "Many of them were crying with us, and they were still and quiet. I like to think they were filled with awe at the Christ that they saw in us as we worshiped and cried together."

A strange thing happened after the brief burial service ended. An old woman standing at the fence began calling out in Arabic.

"Why are you crying?" she shouted.

One of the hospital workers walked over to the fence and said, "What is it, Mama?"

"Why are you crying?" the woman repeated, her eyes aflame. "They are not here! They are not in the ground. They are up in heaven. They were good people."

The worker replied: "If you have seen good in their lives, it's because of Christ's love in them. That's why they are in heaven."

The hospital at Jibla—renamed Peace Hospital—reopened in February 2003 under the administration of Yemen's government health ministry.

It operated at a much smaller capacity for months. There were difficult days as it struggled to regain the high level of care it had provided for so many years. But the fact that it reopened at all was a miracle to those who serve there.

"God moved to reopen it," said one hospital worker at the time.

Whether the hospital would continue operation had been a major question in the discouraging months before the killings. But in the aftermath of the attack, the government pledged to keep the hospital open, appointed a Yemeni administrator and nursing director with long experience at Jibla—and reaffirmed that Southern Baptists and other Christian medical workers could continue serving alongside their Yemeni colleagues.

By mid-2004, the hospital was treating as many outpatients (about 150 a day) as it had at its height, and performing about 600 surgeries a month. Its 50 beds once again were full most of the time.

Pharmacist Don Caswell fully recovered from his wounds. He didn't return to Jibla, but continued to serve with his wife, Teri, and their children elsewhere in the region for nearly two years.

Marty Koehn did return to Jibla (in early 2003) after spending some time with her adult children in the United States. She was still there nearly two years later, far beyond the date she had originally planned to retire.

"My role in Yemen today is to model God's love to people who need to know Him in a personal way," she says. "I feel everybody is watching closely everything I do."

That's why she wrote to the president of Yemen, appealing for mercy for the man who killed her husband. Abed Abdul Razak Kamel, convicted of murdering Bill, Martha, and Kathy, was sentenced in mid-2003 to die for the crime. The sentence was appealed to Yemen's highest court, which upheld it. However, by late 2004 the execution still had not been carried out.

"I asked for the death sentence to be commuted to life imprison-

ment," Marty explains. "I have had no direct response from the president, but to date the killer has not been executed. This was the act of a single person who truly believed he was carrying out God's will in murdering Christians. The man was not from Jibla and did not really know Bill, Martha, and Kathy. The local people were as shocked and horrified as we were. They have bent over backward to look after me and try to make it up to me."

Some Yemenis expressed a preference for rougher justice. A powerful sheik, who admired the slain trio, informed a hospital worker he had asked the authorities to carry out the death sentence slowly—with a pair of scissors.

"He thought that would please me, since it's an 'eye for an eye' in Yemeni culture," the worker relates. "But I said, 'No, we don't want this man executed at all. Because Jesus has forgiven us, we must forgive others.' "

The sheik's basic response: "You Christians are crazy!"

The Yemenis who helped Marty translate her written appeal into Arabic, however, were moved to tears by her expression of forgiveness.

Such interactions reveal the continuing movement of God in Jibla —and beyond.

"We're seeing a movement of the Holy Spirit," says one worker. "I believe it's because the blood of the martyrs cries out from the ground."

The impact of three lives given wholly to Christ—and wholly to Yemen—will reverberate there for generations to come.

BILL HYDE

big guy, big vision

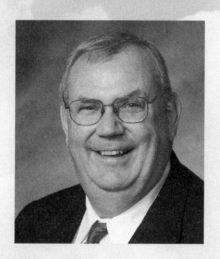

4

Bill Hyde

"Then the eleven disciples went to Galilee, to the mountain where Jesus had told them to go …." (Matthew 28:16, NIV).

March 4, 2003 …

It started as a typical day for missionaries Bill and Lyn Hyde, 25-year veterans of ministry in the Philippines.

Up at 4:30 a.m. Prayer at their home in Davao City on the southern island of Mindanao. It was their most cherished time of the day—and often their only time alone. Then Lyn began her day's work preparing to speak at an upcoming women's conference. Bill jumped in his vehicle for a long day trip to an isolated part of Mindanao, where he planned to meet with a group of Filipino church starters.

Mindanao has endured decades of fighting between government troops and Muslim separatist groups in certain areas. Bill was on the way to one such trouble spot. It had seen frequent kidnappings and a recent increase in skirmishes between rebels and the military.

"I asked him whether it was too dangerous for him to go," Lyn recalls.

"Don't worry," Bill assured her. "It'll be fine. I'll be back in time to pick up Mark and Barbara at the airport."

Mark and Barbara Stevens, the Hydes' neighbors and fellow missionaries, were returning by plane that evening with their two young children from Manila, the Philippine capital. Bill and Lyn were well-

known for being at the airport in Davao to welcome arriving missionaries and drive them home, where a meal cooked by Lyn usually waited
on the table.

Bill got back late that afternoon, safe and sound but dog-tired after
11 hours on the road. Lyn offered to drive to the airport to meet the Stevens family if Bill would handle the Tuesday evening prayer gathering
at church, part of Lyn's prayer ministry.

"Nah, you're the spiritual one," teased a weary Bill, always the joker.
"You go to prayer meeting; I'll go to the airport. I'll see you later."

And so he went. In all their years on Mindanao, it was the first
time they hadn't driven together on an "airport run."

The Stevenses' plane arrived on time. Barbara walked outside the
airport terminal with 4-year-old Sarah beside her and 10-month-old
Nathan in her arms, while Mark waited for their luggage. Bill stood
smiling and waving under a wooden shelter with a crowd of Filipinos
waiting for family members and friends. The sky darkened with approaching rain, so Bill handed Barbara the keys and urged her to walk
on to the car while he helped Mark with the luggage. Barbara hesitated.

"It's OK," Bill insisted. "You and the kids don't have to stand here
and wait with me."

Barbara, Sarah, and Nathan headed for the car. They were perhaps 30 feet away from Bill when a blast detonated behind them and
a blinding flash filled the area. A bomb hidden in a bag left under the
waiting shelter had exploded—directly behind Bill and only a few
yards away. Flying shrapnel hit Barbara in several places; a shard of
hot metal pierced Nathan's liver.

Amid the screaming, smoke, and confusion, Barbara—bleeding
and nearly in shock—didn't know if another blast was coming.

Fueled by adrenaline and a mother's protective instinct, she ran to the car with her crying children in her arms and called Lyn from her cell phone.

"There's been a bomb!" she screamed when Lyn answered. "The kids and I are hurt. I don't know where Bill and Mark are."

> "THERE'S BEEN A BOMB! THE KIDS AND I ARE HURT. I DON'T KNOW WHERE BILL AND MARK ARE."

Lyn urged her to get out of the area and drive directly to a hospital. At first, it didn't occur to her that Bill might be hurt, too—even when he didn't answer repeated calls to his cell phone. "Where are you, Bill?" she wondered, a bit irritated. "Answer the phone. This is an emergency!"

Then another call came. "Lyn, there's been a bomb at the airport," another missionary said. "Get to the hospital. Bill is hurt." She rushed to Davao Doctors Hospital, where Barbara had gone, and comforted Barbara and the children in the emergency room. Barbara's injuries were painful but fairly minor. Nathan later fully recovered, though he was in serious condition for several days.

Bomb victims kept arriving at the hospital, but Bill wasn't there.

Meanwhile, Mark Stevens—unharmed by the blast—had run out of the terminal to witness a scene of panic, injured people screaming for help, and other victims lying dead in widening pools of blood. While desperately searching for his family, he spotted Bill on the pavement— face up, eyes open. Countless pieces of shrapnel riddled Bill's 250- pound body. He had taken almost the full force of the bomb blast— which probably saved the lives of several others in front of him.

He was still alive. When Mark knelt at his side, Bill managed to raise his forearm and grasp his friend's hand in a tight grip. He couldn't speak.

"Hang on, Bill," Mark whispered, softly patting the wounded missionary's face.

HIS EYES WERE CLOSED. WHEN SHE SPOKE SOFTLY TO HIM THEY OPENED, AND LOOKED INTO HERS. THEN THEY CLOSED AGAIN.

A police van arrived. Five men lifted Bill inside and the van raced off. They took him to a government hospital while Mark continued searching for Barbara and the kids. Another missionary arriving on the scene told him his family had gone to Doctors Hospital, where he quickly joined them.

It took nearly an hour for Lyn and other missionaries to locate Bill. As they rushed to the government hospital with Filipino friends, Lyn felt God clearly talking to her. He spoke in the merciful words of Joseph in Genesis 50:20 to his needy brothers, who had cruelly sold him to slavers bound for Egypt: "You intended to harm me, but God intended it for good to accomplish what is now being done, the saving of many lives" (NIV).

"I spoke it out loud to everybody in the car," Lyn relates. "I said, 'The Lord is telling me that regardless of what happens, more people are going to come to know Christ as a result of this.'"

More than 100 bombing victims lay injured in the emergency area of the government hospital. As soon as Lyn came to Bill's side, she knew he wouldn't survive. His eyes were closed. When she spoke softly to him they opened, and looked into hers. Then they closed again.

"I told him that since he had opened his eyes, I knew he could hear me, even though he couldn't speak. He opened his eyes again, and I continued talking to him until I was instructed to leave."

Lyn stepped back as Filipino medical workers surrounded Bill and struggled to keep him alive. They had already warned her that he had only a one-in-100 chance of survival. He slipped away soon after she left his side.

The bomb at Davao City's airport, planted by a member of one of Mindanao's Muslim rebel groups, injured more than 150 Filipinos. It killed 23 people—including one American, a 59-year-old Southern Baptist missionary named Bill Hyde.

It's ironic that Bill Hyde died at the little airport he'd walked through countless times over the years. If not for the tragedy of the event, Bill himself might have smiled at the thought of meeting deadly violence at such a mundane location.

Here's a guy who made a habit of going into some of the most dangerous places in the Philippines. Places risky even to drive to over bad roads—or no road. Places where you could get kidnapped, shot at, or worse—especially if you were a foreigner. He'd just returned from such a place that day.

"Bill was never afraid to go anywhere in the Philippines," Lyn says. "Until March 4, no one thought of the airport as a 'soft target' for a terrorist bombing. Until March 4, Davao City was considered a safe place in Mindanao."

But why did Bill willingly go into all those other dangerous places? After surviving the Vietnam War more than 30 years before, he once vowed never to leave the United States again.

To understand his change of heart, you need to travel back in time.

William P. Hyde was born February 3, 1944. He grew up in Shellsburg, a small farming town in Iowa, the home state he shared with his movie hero, John Wayne. The youngest of three children, Bill was a big, athletic Iowa farm kid with a ready smile—and ready fists if the situation demanded.

"HIS NICKNAME WAS 'SLUGGER.' HE GOT INTO LOTS OF FIGHTS."

"His nickname was 'Slugger,' " his older brother Dick remembers. "He got into lots of fights."

Bill had a strong will and a fiery competitive streak from the beginning. But he wasn't a bully. Fighting was the way boys proved themselves in those days. Big guys like Bill (and John Wayne) attracted frequent attention from young upstarts looking to make a name for themselves in a showdown.

Mostly, Bill proved himself in sports. They came naturally to him—especially basketball and baseball. When he wasn't working at his father's hardware and farm implement store, he starred in both sports in high school. He collected a batch of individual and team awards along the way, and later earned a basketball scholarship to college.

Bill was anything but a one-dimensional jock, though. His competitive instinct extended to all games—including chess, perhaps the supreme test of concentration and strategic thinking. To this he added a voracious appetite for knowledge.

> "HE KNEW ELECTRONICS, COMPUTERS, RADIO COMMUNICATIONS, THEOLOGY, HISTORY, MUSIC, MECHANICAL. YOU NAME IT, HE SEEMED TO KNOW ABOUT IT—IN-DEPTH."

"One of the amazing things about Bill was how much he knew about so many things," says a missionary colleague and close friend in the Philippines. "I remember him saying that when he was in school he never followed the lesson plans or listened to the teacher. He sat at the back of the room by the encyclopedias and just read through them, volume after volume. He knew electronics, computers, radio communications, theology, history, music, mechanical. You name it, he seemed to know about it—in-depth."

The zeal for knowledge stayed with him, along with the love of games. In later years, says missionary Diana Clark, "I could almost see Bill looking at the world like a giant 'Risk' game—thinking of how the most people could come to Christ in the shortest possible time."

How did Bill himself meet Christ? He grew up in a Methodist family and attended a solid evangelical Federated church (half the congregation was Methodist, half was Baptist). He accepted Christ as his personal Savior at age 12 during a Vacation Bible School, and later renewed his life commitment as a young adult during college in Iowa City, where he was baptized at Bethany Baptist Church.

Another God-given talent emerged during Bill's early teenage years: music. The Hydes were a musical family; everybody sang. But Bill's voice came out in an off-key monotone—at first.

"My older brother and I wouldn't let him sing with us," sister Barbara admits with a laugh. "In those days we three kids washed the dishes in a dishpan sitting on a table. We'd sing together, but we just hated to have Bill sing with us, because he couldn't sing!"

That soon changed. Bill started studying music and playing trumpet in high school. He kept singing, too, on the side. He made his solo "debut" at Barbara's wedding, unveiling a rich bass voice that sounded like Tennessee Ernie Ford. It amazed everyone.

Music eventually overtook sports on Bill's priority list. After starting at Upper Iowa University on a basketball scholarship, he transferred to the University of Iowa in Iowa City, where he eventually earned bachelor and master's degrees in music and choral literature. While attending Bethany Baptist Church near the university, he accepted a part-time job directing the choir—and met Garlinda (Lyn) Gage, an attractive young woman singing in the alto section.

Lyn needed a ride home from choir practices; Bill was more than happy to oblige. Their friendship quickly bloomed.

"Persistence led to a date," Bill later wryly observed. "Then engagement. And on June 12, 1966, Garlinda Gage became Mrs. Bill Hyde."

Their early months of married life revolved around the church and college studies, which they planned to finish together. But the U.S. Army intervened with a draft notice—and the Vietnam War awaited. Bill trained as a radio operator and was stationed in Da

Nang at the height of U.S. military involvement in 1967-68.

Like a lot of veterans, Bill never said much about what he saw and experienced during his term in Vietnam. He suffered no physical wounds, but he brought home unseen scars.

When he returned, Bill stepped off the plane in his military uniform, carrying a small bag. The only "souvenir" inside the bag: a large piece of shrapnel. One night during a mortar attack on his camp, the shrapnel had ripped through the top of his tent—and through the center of his cot, where he had been lying only minutes before.

"God had spared Bill's life," says Lyn. "We didn't know why, but we were thankful that for him the war was over. When Bill returned from the war, he informed me that he would never leave the United States again."

> "WHEN BILL RETURNED FROM THE WAR, HE INFORMED ME THAT HE WOULD NEVER LEAVE THE UNITED STATES AGAIN."

Bill grudgingly amended that vow later: *"IF* I ever leave the United States again, it definitely won't be to Southeast Asia."

End of discussion—or so he thought.

THE HOOK IS SET

Busy years followed. Bill taught music and choir in public schools to a variety of age groups. Two sons, Tim and Steve, arrived. Bill and Lyn devoted their summers to local volunteer mission work and trips to mountains of the American West. They combined their love of kids, ministry, and the great outdoors in directing Iowa's Pine Lake Baptist Camp for a year. All the while, Bill maintained his school teaching schedule.

The high point of those years: a 1975 summer of missions in Alaska, where the couple helped build and lead a wilderness Bible camp. For Bill it was an ideal setting. He loved the vast open spaces, the mountains and forests, the brisk northern air, the chance to minister to young people. He dreamed of spending the rest of his life there.

"Bill would take zero-degree weather any day over temperatures above 70" says Lyn. "We were revived and our spirits uplifted being in the presence of our Creator in these beautifully magnificent locations. Before we made the trip with our two sons (then ages 3 and 4), Bill had decided that if he could find a teaching job while we were in Alaska, we would stay and make our home there."

But God was using the experience to prepare him for something else.

Lyn: "The summer in Alaska was the first time we had actually been away from our home roots as a family for any length of time. It was the first time we had to face loneliness in its simplest form and work with other short-termers for an extended period. It was a life-changing experience for us all. The 'hook' of missions was set. My call to missions had come when I was a child. For Bill, the call to missions was a process over time as the Lord continued to open his mind and heart to the possibilities that awaited him."

The teaching job in Alaska came through. But the Lord was already revealing to Bill the great north wouldn't be his destination.

He turned down the job. He knew he was giving up something he deeply desired, but an even deeper desire was emerging.

"Bill's favorite verse in the Bible was Matthew 28:16, which says, 'Then the eleven disciples went to Galilee, to the mountain where Jesus had told them to go,'" Lyn explains. "The verses we know as the Great Commission follow. Bill lived by this passage and emphasized it over and over again wherever he spoke. He would tell people that if they went where Jesus told them to go, they would be able to carry out the Great Commission in those places where He wants them to be."

For Bill and Lyn, that meant seeking missionary appointment through the Southern Baptist Foreign (now International) Mission Board. They considered missionary assignments in five different countries. Only one location offered a match for their gifts: the Philippines.

Was God giving Bill an opportunity to live out his favorite verse by calling him back to Southeast Asia—a place of stifling heat and humidity, a place of painful war memories, the one place in the world where he didn't want to go?

If there were any doubt, the Lord supplied two more key verses to the couple as they prayed and sought His direction:

1. "Sing to the Lord a new song, His praise from the ends of the earth, you who go down to the sea, and all that is in it, you islands, and all who live in them" (Isaiah 42:10, NIV).

2. "If I rise on the wings of the dawn, if I settle on the far side of the sea, even there your hand will guide me, your right hand will hold me fast" (Psalm 139:9,10, NIV).

The ends of the earth. The far side of the sea. Islands, and a new song of praise to be sung by all who live in them. The Philippines.

"SING TO THE LORD A NEW SONG, HIS PRAISE FROM THE ENDS OF THE EARTH, YOU WHO GO DOWN TO THE SEA, AND ALL THAT IS IN IT, YOU ISLANDS, AND ALL WHO LIVE IN THEM" (ISAIAH 42:10, NIV).

The Hydes were appointed missionaries in 1978. Their first assignment fit their skills and experience perfectly: teaching at Faith Academy, a school for children of missionaries near Manila. They spent 11 productive years there shaping young lives, including their own sons. Never one to stay inside the bounds of walls and programs, Bill seldom missed an opportunity to take students and choir groups on mission trips around the country.

He first encountered the adventure of church starting while working on weekends with the late Jack Branan, a veteran missionary church planter. As Jack and his wife, Rosanne, mentored the younger couple, a wider vision for reaching the lost began to form in Bill's ever-active mind. He sensed God leading him toward a new task—teaching Filipinos studying theology at Southern Baptist College in M'lang, on the island of Mindanao.

To meet the new assignment's requirements, Bill obtained a master of divinity degree at Southwestern Baptist Theological Seminary in Forth Worth during one missionary furlough—a marathon-like feat. In M'lang, Bill and Lyn came under the wing of another great missionary couple: Thurman and Kathie Braughton.

"Thurman and Kathie had a powerful influence on our lives," says Lyn. "We learned how to love Filipinos into the kingdom, how to be the kind of missionaries who would have a ministry that stands the test of time."

Bill also learned a lot more about starting churches from Braughton, another veteran church planter. At the college, meanwhile, Bill did more than teach Filipino students called to spread the gospel; he began pouring his life into them.

His language skills weren't very good; he hadn't needed to learn Tagalog (the primary language of most Filipinos) to teach English-speaking missionary kids at Faith Academy. By now he was well into middle age—a tough time to strengthen language ability. He studied hard, but he never became truly fluent.

Bill had something else, however, that bridged any communication gap with young Filipinos: unconditional commitment to them.

"He had a passion to equip Filipinos for ministry and leadership," says former missionary Don Phelps, another long-time friend and Philippines co-worker. "On the weekends he would go out and invest himself in their lives and ministries. He had such a rapport with them; he was a natural at spending time with them and encouraging them."

That extended far beyond students at the college and local pastors. Bill would go anywhere.

"There was no place that was too hard to get to, or too inconvenient," Phelps says. "He would just go, and he would load up his truck with Filipino pastors and lay people he'd take with him. He didn't expect people to come to him. He knew not everybody could come to the Baptist seminary or the college. So he would go where they were."

From that "seedbed" of teaching and encouraging ministers, a grand vision began to grow inside Bill: to equip believers to train other believers, to equip churches to start new churches, to multiply the gospel throughout Mindanao—and beyond.

> "THERE WAS NO PLACE THAT WAS TOO HARD TO GET TO, OR TOO INCONVENIENT. HE WOULD JUST GO, AND HE WOULD LOAD UP HIS TRUCK WITH FILIPINO PASTORS AND LAY PEOPLE HE'D TAKE WITH HIM."

The ground was prepared for the full blooming of Bill's life mission.

"JOHN WAYNE THEOLOGY"

In 1997 the Hydes transferred to Davao City, and Bill began to focus all his energies on training church planters. By this time he was a man with a plan. Just ask him; he'd tell you—in no uncertain terms.

"Bill was convinced that his way was the right way," recalls Barbara Stevens, one of many missionaries who joined (or was drafted into) Bill's informal "debate society" over the years.

"We didn't always agree, but he was one of those guys who you could tell, 'Bill, you're dead wrong!' … and it was OK."

He relished the give-and-take of lively conversation—especially when it came to mission strategy. You had to stand your ground, though.

Like John Wayne, his fellow Iowan whose tough-guy movie characters seldom suffered self-doubt, Bill knew his mind.

"Bill could be kind of intimidating until you got to know him," says a missionary friend. "He was tall and barrel-chested, with a deep voice that boomed with authority and confidence. We spent many nights playing Mexican dominoes, which Bill generally dominated since his mind seemed to work on a different level than the rest of us. He had an extensive collection of John Wayne movies, and we would always want to watch the Westerns while our wives would want more 'sensitive' selections. Bill even developed a theory on how John Wayne had influenced American theology. I don't remember the details, but to hear Bill explain it, it made a lot of sense.

"Bill himself was much like an 'apostolic John Wayne,' especially when you saw him in the Filipino context doing what God called him to do. Aside from the physical similarities, he approached life

"BILL HIMSELF WAS MUCH LIKE AN APOSTOLIC JOHN WAYNE. ... HE TOOK ON THE DEVIL AND REFUSED TO ACCEPT DEFEAT, WITH A VISION TO EXPAND THE KINGDOM THAT WAS AS BIG AS THE WEST."

and ministry in a similar way. He took on the devil and refused to accept defeat, with a vision to expand the kingdom that was as big as the West. As big as Bill was, he was doing something that was bigger than himself."

Even when it came to the mission organization, Bill "just didn't fit into a nice, organized, limited structure," the missionary adds.

"People would say, 'Now Bill, this is your area of responsibility and you need to stay within these geographical boundaries and this people group focus.' Bill would look at the map and see the whole island of Mindanao and feel responsible to reach all of it and beyond to all of the Philippines and the world.

"The amazing thing was that it wasn't just vision and talk. Bill was doing it."

How?

Well, he may have admired John Wayne and the rugged cowboy individualism of the Old West, but he was no Lone Ranger. For all his opinionated exuberance, Bill carefully listened to his "debate" partners and others, taking mental notes. He inhaled new ideas from many sources—and used them. The curiosity he'd always displayed—from his early days reading encyclopedias in the back of class to his passion for chess strategies—stayed keen.

One of the key later influences on Bill's approach to training church planters came from his own son, Steve—now grown and serving as a missionary elsewhere in Asia. The Hydes visited Steve in the restricted country where he works, observed him in action and questioned him about his methods and materials.

"The next time Steve came to our place, he was looking at some of Bill's training materials, and they were exact copies," Lyn reports. "It was hilarious. Steve really enjoyed that—that his Dad had actually learned something from him and copied it, and it was working!"

The key to Bill's church-planting strategy was simple: like the Apostle Paul, he multiplied himself in other faithful men, who could in turn multiply themselves in others.

He started by training a core group of seven Filipino men committed to church planting. As they became trainers, the circle widened into what became a network of hundreds.

He never went anywhere alone. He always took at least one young Filipino or missionary—and usually as many as he could pack into his vehicle—on his constant trips into the hinterlands. He trained Filipinos to start churches, then let them take the lead while he went along to observe and encourage. He expected application—and results. He followed up to see if theory was becoming reality.

Most importantly, he flatly refused to do anything in ministry leadership that Filipino believers could do themselves.

"He trained pastors and lay people in spiritual disciplines, from keeping a quiet time to leading a Bible study," says Don Phelps. "He taught evangelism skills. It was very practical. It wasn't book-intensive. They would use the Bible as their textbook. He would give them assignments and expect them to do it. He didn't want people just to sit and listen. He wanted them to apply what they were learning in ministry."

HE TRAINED FILIPINOS TO START CHURCHES, THEN LET THEM TAKE THE LEAD. HE FLATLY REFUSED TO DO ANYTHING IN MINISTRY LEADERSHIP THAT FILIPINO BELIEVERS COULD DO THEMSELVES.

He would go from one church association to another, then another, then back to the first to check on progress. He equipped leaders to go where he couldn't—tribal areas, isolated hometowns and villages—and set 'em loose.

There were no Motel 6's leaving the light on in the places Bill and his crew usually visited.

"They traveled together, ate together, worked and slept together," Lyn explains. "Camping and backpacking were things Bill enjoyed in his younger years, but the church-planting training Bill conducted with 'his men' in the tropical heat of the Philippines was far different than the cool mountain ranges in the States. They usually slept on a narrow bench, or a cement or bamboo floor. It was always too hot for a mosquito net, so putting up with the elements and the critters was all part of the experience."

After one particularly exhausting trek, Bill came home and declared to Lyn, "I'm getting too old for this!" He'd trained all the previous day in the heat, then tried to get some sleep on a bamboo floor in the sweltering darkness. After slapping at the mosquitoes buzzing around his face for a while, he grabbed the shirt he had stripped off and put it over his head—only to discover the shirt was filled with ants.

Such were the joys of "camping with Bill." But he kept at it. At home, meanwhile, Bill and Lyn stayed available and on call for "his men"—and their wives, whom Lyn ministered to and encouraged.

"The men and their families had access to our home and us at any time of the day or night," Lyn says. "They knew they could come to us with their joys and sorrows, their problems, and celebrations. I maintained our home with open hospitality, feeding and sleeping any number of people who would arrive unannounced any day of the week."

One of those Filipino men was Eddie Palingcod, a member of Bill's original group of seven trainers/church planters. He met Bill in 1998 through their mutual friend, missionary Thurman Braughton.

The two spent so much time together that Eddie became known in some circles as "Bill Junior."

Eddie lacked education, but more than made up for it in evangelistic passion. Working with Bill, he became the leading Baptist church-planting trainer for an entire province in the Philippines, Davao del Norte.

Bill's approach departed from the traditional idea of missionaries—or national pastors—starting one church at a time, Eddie stresses:

"He said to me, 'Eddie, you need to train others to plant churches. It's not that you're doing the wrong thing now, but you need to multiply.' It was hard for me to understand at first, but when I applied it, I got excited."

Eddie learned not only to win new believers and baptize them, but to disciple them, to form evangelism teams, prayer teams, disciple-making and church-planting teams to reach out farther.

"Bill always said, 'Plan the work and work the plan,'" Eddie recalls. "He also said, 'Focus on the ministry, not the position.'"

The point: not just to achieve the honored office of pastor or "professional" church worker, but to multiply the gospel.

Some of Eddie's trainers took offense at that challenge, he admits. "They said, 'This missionary is very frank'"—maybe too frank. "But to me this word is precious. It is very simple, but very precious. Even though he is now living in heaven, I told Bill, 'It works!'"

Today, Eddie has lifted his vision beyond the lowland areas, where he did most of his work with Bill, to the uplands of Mindanao, where tribal peoples live. But he still uses the same methods he learned from his friend. Every month, he journeys into the mountains to visit and encourage 17 church-planting trainers.

In perhaps the crowning effort of his missionary service, Bill organized a major evangelism training conference only a few months before he died. He invited Southern Baptist missionary Wade Akins, who trains pioneer evangelists around the world, to lead sessions in three cities. Akins was amazed by the turnout—and the conference locations.

"He had almost 4,000 attend the training—the largest church-planting training I know of anywhere in the world," Wade says. "He had 150 coordinators ready for all the follow-up, and we formed 1,081 church-planting teams. We went to three different venues because no one place would hold all those people. One of the places was a strong Islamic area. They had bodyguards everywhere. I couldn't even cross the street without bodyguards, and they circled the arena."

Wade noticed something else. Through two weeks together and numerous conference sessions, Bill never once took the stage—or the spotlight:

"He never got up. He never said a thing unless he was asked to. He let the Filipinos run the whole show. He would sit in the middle of the audience. He was the man behind it, but you never would have known it. To me that was an expression of humility. A lot of guys would want to be up there taking credit. I never saw any of that in him."

Wade did, however, encounter Bill's competitive fire before one of the evening conferences. Wade likes to play chess and brought a little set with him to take on Bill.

"He was warning me that he'd played for 30 years, that he played every night on the computer," Wade recounts with a grin. "I said, 'Well, I'm not all that good but I'll try ya.' I figured I was going to get slaughtered, but I beat him!

"Then I looked at my watch and saw the meeting was going to start in 10 minutes. We had about 2,000 people waiting in a sports arena, so I said, 'Bill, we better get on down there.' Bill said, 'Oh no you don't. We're going to play another game!' We got to the meeting late."

And Bill won the second game.

WORTH DYING FOR

Those last months were among the happiest of their married lives for Bill and Lyn. Bill had worked hard in recent years to spend more time at home, moderating some of his workaholic tendencies that had created strain in the past. They cherished times of prayer together and were enjoying the renewed friendship of the "empty nest" years.

They also were able to spend time with both of their sons. They had visited Steve and his young family for several weeks in his Asian mission field of service at the end of 2002 and into the new year. Tim, active in a church in Texas, had come to Mindanao in January to work for two weeks on a ministry team.

"I can look back and see the many ways the Lord was preparing us, though we didn't know it," Lyn reflects. "So many times as I was sitting with Bill, the thought would occur to me, 'Can it get any better than this?'"

Something Bill said near the end of his life would also comfort

Lyn after his death. When they visited Steve on his mission field, their son had said of his newly adopted nation: "Sometime, I'm either going to retire here or die here. But I'm not going to leave these people until they come to know Christ."

Those words affected Bill deeply. Later that day, he told Lyn, "My son is willing to die for the people of this country. I had to ask myself: Am I willing to die for the Filipino people? And my answer is yes."

> "SOMETIME, I'M EITHER GOING TO RETIRE HERE OR DIE HERE. BUT I'M NOT GOING TO LEAVE THESE PEOPLE UNTIL THEY COME TO KNOW CHRIST."

Only weeks later, he did just that.

A few days after his death, the family placed a wreath alongside many others at the small crater left at the site of the airport bombing. A banner on the wreath said: "From The Bill Hyde family and Americans who love Filipinos and know that they are worth dying for."

POSTSCRIPT: BILL'S LEGACIES

What is Bill Hyde's legacy? He actually leaves multiple legacies, and they continue to thrive and grow. Bill's vision lives:

- in the hundreds of churches started through his ministry of multiplication and the thousands that will come from them. "This guy took what we were doing and multiplied it tenfold, maybe a hundredfold," says his missionary mentor, Thurman Braughton. "Where we were adding, he was multiplying."

- in the thousands of lost Filipinos won to Christ.

- in the ongoing ministries of young missionaries he mentored and encouraged, like Mark and Barbara Stevens. After surviving the bombing, the Stevenses experienced their most productive year yet in reaching out to tribal groups in the Philippines.
- in the ministry of his life partner, Lyn, who courageously returned to the Philippines in early 2004 after a time of recovery and seeking God's will. Bill would love her new mission

"ALTHOUGH A TERRORIST BOMB KILLED MY HUSBAND, I KNEW IT HAD NOT KILLED GOD'S CALL ON MY LIFE."

assignment: challenging and training Filipino churches to send out their own missionaries, whether in the Philippines or around the world. "I miss Bill terribly," she readily acknowledges. "We ache tremendously for our personal loss. Life is not the same without Bill. He paid the ultimate sacrifice for his commitment to Christ. But we know that his life was not wasted. And although a terrorist bomb killed my husband, I knew it had not killed God's call on my life." She prays that her new ministry might one day even send Filipinos to reach those who killed Bill, and train them how to give life, not take it.

- in the lives of his sons, who are following in his footsteps. At his father's funeral service in Iowa, Steve said: "I will avenge my father's death. Not by killing or violence: I'll go into this world and shine the light of Jesus into dark places."

- perhaps most of all, in the lives of hundreds of godly Filipino men like Eddie Palingcod, who continue to live out the passion for church-multiplying Bill instilled in them.

"Every day I read the Bible Bill gave me before he died," says Eddie, now 39. "He was my discipler, but he was also just like a father. After his death, it was hard to continue. But at his memorial service, I told him in my heart, 'Bill, I will continue.'

"Bill died, but his ministry is still alive."

IRAQ PROLOGUE

They had given so much—and had so much more to give.

David and Carrie McDonnall spent several adventure-packed years as single workers in the Middle East, where they met in Bethlehem at the turn of the millennium. They had returned to the region together as a young married couple—called by God to love Arabs, eager to help Iraqis rebuild their lives.

Larry and Jean Elliott had given a quarter-century serving the poor of Honduras through relief and development ministries, church starting—and one-by-one love and compassion. They had come to Iraq only weeks before, excited to put their long experience to full use for needy Iraqis.

Karen Watson had come to Iraq among the first wave of relief workers, toiling long and hard to get Southern Baptist aid projects going in a dangerous, chaotic environment. After several months in a nearby country, she had just returned, ready to continue her courageous work.

But all their skill and experience, all their energetic willingness to serve—and four of their lives—came to an abrupt end March 15, 2004, on a road near Mosul, Iraq.

They were tired but enthusiastic after a day of surveying potential water purification projects. Iraqis, thirsty for clean water, had welcomed them warmly and asked them to return soon. But as they drove near the city, they were attacked by nameless killers who pulled alongside their truck and riddled it with gunfire. The Elliotts and Karen Watson died almost immediately. David McDonnall, wounded but still mobile, got help for his critically injured wife. He, too, later died.

Carrie McDonnall would wake up days later in a Texas hospital, facing months of rehabilitation—and the shattering news that her husband was gone.

But Carrie wasn't defeated that violent day in Iraq.

Nor were David, Karen, Larry, or Jean. They died the way they lived: victoriously.

DAVID McDONNALL

the adventures of 'dangerous dave'

5

He went places where no outsider had dared go before to share the gospel.

He navigated minefields and dodged civil wars to find lost villages.

He got arrested in three countries for telling people about Jesus.

He hung out with Bedouins and desert tribesmen, who were among his best friends.

He loved the majestic mountains of Colorado, where he grew up, and the trackless desert wilderness of North Africa, his adopted home.

He transformed the lives of more people in a few years of ministry than most Christians ever meet.

And he enjoyed almost every minute of it. For David McDonnall, life was a grand adventure.

Attention young thrill seekers, edge walkers, and explorers of the extreme: This story is for you.

If you've ever risked your life just to feel the adrenaline rush, you don't understand how precious life is. David McDonnall understood life's priceless value; he savored each moment. Yet he risked his life more than once—and ultimately gave it up on a dusty road in Iraq— for one great purpose: the glory of God among the nations.

Some risk takers have a secret death wish. David, on the other hand, had a powerful and public *life wish*, overflowing with laughter and joy, excited about the possibilities of each day, intoxicated with the love of Jesus. Like the Apostle Paul, he was an unashamed fool for Christ—and just as willing to face danger for the gospel's sake.

DAVID MCDONNALL, IN THE WORDS OF ONE ADMIRER, PRESENTED HIMSELF AS AN "EXUBERANT SACRIFICE" ON THE ALTAR OF GOD.

David's approach to living also recalls the first David, his biblical namesake. Not the King David of later years—who struggled with sin, palace intrigue, and the burdens of rule—but the young David. The David who slew lions and bears, who met Goliath on the field of battle with nothing but a slingshot and a rash trust in God, who danced and sang praises to the Lord with all his might.

David McDonnall, in the words of one admirer, presented himself as an "exuberant sacrifice" on the altar of God.

Here is a brief glimpse into his life.

BUSTING OUT

Some folks refuse to believe it, but there was a time when David McDonnall was shy.

"In high school, he was very quiet," confirms his mother, Donna McDonnall. "He didn't make friends easily. He had two or three close friends that he spent a lot of time with."

He was still on the quiet side when he arrived in 1993 on the campus of West Texas A&M University in Canyon, Texas. Shawn Macklin, two years older, lived just down the hall in David's dormitory. He noticed the freshman from Colorado seemed a bit intimidated by some of the heavy-duty party guys on the floor. Shawn, a committed Christian, took the new kid under his wing.

"He was kind of a loner," Shawn remembers. "I felt like he was searching for friends. I had a pretty good network, so I started inviting him to go on group outings. Then he got heavily involved in the Baptist Student Ministries, where I'd already been active."

When did David come out of his shell? Hard to say for sure. Some think it was during a college mission trip to New Mexico. Others claim it was the night the movie projector broke down at a local theater in Canyon. David amazed everybody by jumping onstage to entertain the audience with goofy antics until the movie resumed.

WHEN HIS SHELL CRACKED, IT SHATTERED
—AND A WILD AND CRAZY NEW DAVE BURST
ONTO AN UNSUSPECTING A&M CAMPUS.

Maybe he was just a late bloomer, delighting in finding his niche in college life. In any case, when his shell cracked, it shattered—and a wild and crazy new Dave burst onto an unsuspecting A&M campus.

"It was like, 'Whoa, we didn't know what was inside of this guy!'" Shawn admits. "A lot of people didn't know what to think at first. But by the time he graduated, I don't think there was a person in Canyon who didn't know him. He was one of those people you couldn't meet without being changed in some way"—almost always for the better.

But that's getting ahead of the story.

David Edwin McDonnall was born February 24, 1975, in Colorado Springs, the first child of Bruce and Donna McDonnall (and later the big brother of Danny and Sara Beth). Bruce McDonnall worked as a civil engineer for the Colorado Department of Transportation, so the family moved around the state—first to Aurora and later to Lamar, where David and his siblings attended middle and high school. In each location, the family became a vital part of local Baptist churches.

"Y'all need to know that, as a kid, I had a drug problem," David would solemnly inform listeners decades later. "Every time the church doors opened, my parents drug me to church."

Unlike some kids, however, he enjoyed being 'drug.' At the ripe age of 7, David invited Jesus Christ to be his Lord and Savior. He experienced plenty of spiritual struggles later, as all young Christians do. But that decision forever remained the turning point of his life.

"His relationship with Christ from the earliest days was always the number one thing in his life," says his mother.

David developed some serious secondary passions, however—especially anything involving God's great outdoors. He often went hunting with his father and camping with his Uncle Bob and Aunt Bev. He spent several summers as a boy on the family's farm in Nebraska, riding tractors and helping his Uncle Don tag calves.

He avidly participated in 4-H Club for a decade, winning state championships in shooting and photography—an early talent he nurtured alongside writing. Several homemade movies he produced with his buddies—"Indiana Dave and the Lost Soccer Ball," for example—hinted at David's developing taste for adventure.

He went on youth mission trips, attended music and drama camps, played clarinet, sang in the chorus, and edited the *Savage Chieftain*, Lamar High School's newspaper.

Whatever he had going in school or at church, however, didn't keep him indoors too long.

"Perhaps his greatest anticipation in high school was to get his first 'big game' hunting license at 14," his mother wrote. "The prospect of deer and antelope hunting far overshadowed the typical teen desire for a driver's license. It's difficult to say if David enjoyed stalking animals through the sagebrush with his dad and brother more or less than the pre-dawn ritual of consuming hot chocolate and donuts while waiting for 'shooting light.'

"David loved the mountains of Colorado. He spent many happy hours photographing, fishing, hunting, and hiking throughout the Sangre de Cristos and nearby ranges. He climbed several of the 'fourteeners'"—peaks reaching 14,000 feet or higher.

He especially cherished Lamar First Baptist's annual church retreats at Horn Creek Camp and Conference Center in Westcliffe, Colorado, where he later worked for three summers following high school. He enjoyed hanging out with other workers there, counseling younger campers and pulling off dumb stunts (like shooting at bears with rubber-tipped arrows from the cafeteria roof). It was at Horn Creek that the legend of "Dangerous Dave" was born.

David later wrote about his experiences there in a little book he called Horn Creek Tales. The rugged beauty of the area captured his heart. He was grateful for "the privilege of being able to live and work surrounded by the beauty of God's creation," he reflected. "The mountains around Horn Creek clearly display God's handiwork."

God had other ruggedly beautiful places in mind for this Colorado kid.

CAMPUS GOOFBALL (WITH A PURPOSE)

David excelled in school. He accepted an academic scholarship to West Texas A&M, where he pursued his interest in writing and photography through the university's journalism program.

But Dave himself was the real story around town. When his early shyness melted away, there was just no telling what "Dangerous Dave" might try on campus or in greater Canyon—as long as it was harmless and in good fun.

THERE WAS JUST NO TELLING WHAT "DANGEROUS DAVE" MIGHT TRY ON CAMPUS OR IN GREATER CANYON—AS LONG AS IT WAS HARMLESS AND IN GOOD FUN.

Wanna go swimming? Dave filled the back of his pickup truck with water so his pals could splash around in a mobile pool. Hungry? He greeted finicky eaters in the school cafeteria with chocolate cake smeared on his face.

He often jumped into his pickup with selected buddies and took off on "weekend warrior" trips.

"We'd leave on Friday or Saturday and come home Sunday, sometimes early enough to go to church—or at least to be back in school on Monday," recounts fellow "warrior" David Hale, Dave's college roommate and a friend since Horn Creek days. "It consisted of loading up, taking off, not sleeping, doing stuff, and hanging out."

Dave didn't seem to need that much sleep. He'd stay up all night, knock on dorm room doors, ask buddies to go rappelling or hiking at 3 a.m. "I'd be sound asleep, and I'd have to pass on the chance sometimes," Shawn admits. "Dave just had huge amounts of energy."

If something was outdoors, or slightly off the wall—or both— Dave was all over it.

"He knew how to have fun, how to cut up in the right way and not get involved in all the bad things," explains David Hale. "He had the gift of making people happy. David was never crude or vulgar; he proved you could be hilarious and have a great time without spewing profanities or being immoral. He made others realize that Christianity does not equal boredom. He made them want to do better."

In other words, Dave wasn't just a campus goofball. He was a campus goofball with a purpose. He loved serving people in need— anywhere, anytime.

Once he called Shawn, asking for a helping hand. A blind student was moving into a new dorm room, Dave said, and needed help "moving her Bible." Not for the first time, Shawn questioned Dave's sanity—until he discovered how big a Braille Bible was.

"It was pretty late in the evening and I was really tired, but I went over there with him," Shawn recounts. "I had never seen a Braille Bible before. I didn't realize every book is a huge separate volume of Braille pages. We moved about a truckload of these volumes. David didn't even know the girl that well, but she had heard through the campus grapevine that he was willing to help.

"He was a servant. People were always calling him. It didn't matter what was on his agenda. If somebody needed something, he was there."

Dave's energy, enthusiasm, and emerging leadership skills combined to make him a natural leader for mission trips through the Baptist Student Ministries and First Baptist Church of Canyon. A frequent mission field: South Padre Island, favorite spring break destination for Texas students seeking sun, fun, and alcohol. Dave and his "Beach Reach" team members would hit the beach to tell people about Jesus, offer students safe rides back to their hotels at night, cook free pancake breakfasts for them the next morning.

"He led by example," Shawn says. "When we were doing evangelism, he was always the first one out there visiting with people. He had a lot of courage when it came to sharing his faith. I always enjoyed watching Dave interact with people on the island, because they were from all walks of life."

David began working for the daily *Canyon News* before finishing college. He stayed on with the newspaper after graduation, and got a promotion to news editor. Already a gifted photographer and storyteller, he'd do anything for a good story—and now he had a wider audience. He also remained active at First Baptist in Canyon, teaching and discipling young people.

But he was restless. He hungered for larger challenges. Two crucial experiences during his senior year (1997) had profoundly deepened his commitment to God's purposes—and widened his horizons.

One was the "Walk to Emmaus," a spiritual retreat he attended. Dave came back "on fire," according to a friend at the newspaper. His church and college friends saw the change, too.

After the "Emmaus" retreat, "there was pretty much no doubt

that he was completely giving his life to Christ," David Hale recalls. "Not just his mind and his soul, but his body. We were driving back from a hunting trip and there was a terrible storm, so we pulled over and had a long talk about it. It boiled down to this: He wanted to serve God no matter where, what, or how."

The second experience was a mission trip—this time far beyond Texas. Cliff Lea, then the minister to students at First Baptist in Canyon, invited Dave and some of the other collegians to go to Tanzania in east Africa. They worked with Southern Baptist missionaries in village evangelism for two weeks.

"I think he went for the sport of it at first," Cliff acknowledges. "I'm not saying his motives were skewed, but I don't think he had any intention of maybe becoming a missionary himself. But God really got hold of his life."

Dave returned with a radically deepened commitment to following Christ wherever He led—and a whole new sense of urgency about evangelizing the world. Cliff told him about the Journeyman Program at the International Mission Board, an opportunity for recent college graduates to serve two or three years overseas. Dave checked into it.

At about the same time, Eddie P. (last name omitted for security reasons) was looking for a few adventurous young workers. Eddie, an IMB strategist in Northern Africa and the Middle East, had a daring plan: Send "RASER" teams to wander some of the most difficult, dangerous parts of the region and find openings for the gospel. "RASER" was an acronym for "Remote Area Strategy Evangelist-Researcher."

"Basically the idea was that these guys were going to cut through and go where nobody had ever gone," Eddie explains. "David was the first guy to sign up."

"BASICALLY THE IDEA WAS THAT THESE GUYS WERE GOING TO CUT THROUGH AND GO WHERE NOBODY HAD EVER GONE. DAVID WAS THE FIRST GUY TO SIGN UP."

Dave's parents were concerned about their son's safety—and said so. Eddie spent several hours with them one afternoon discussing the region, the job, the risks.

"If it were up to us, he wouldn't have gone to either place," Donna McDonnall says—not to North Africa, not to Iraq several years later.

"But his father and I are totally convinced that this is where he felt called of the Lord to go."

To Dave's college buddies, the assignment sounded tailor-made.

"I wasn't surprised," Shawn Macklin recalls. "It started making sense to me that through Dave's wacky adventures and all the crazy stuff he'd done, God had been preparing him for a dangerous part of the world. He was nervous, but he felt like that's where he was supposed to be."

Commissioned by the International Mission Board as a journeyman in early 1999, Dave moved to the Northern Africa/Middle East region and began studying Arabic. He picked up the essentials of this difficult language with amazing quickness—and made friends just as quickly. He was gregarious, talkative, funny. Arabs and other Northern Africans loved this friendly guy from America. They instinctively responded to his smile, his laugh, the sparkle in his eyes.

Wherever he went, people remembered him.

"He never met a stranger," insists Chad B., another journeyman who joined the RASER team and became Dave's partner. "He would go somewhere by himself, and a week or two later I'd be there and they'd either call me 'David' or ask me if I knew him. If that happened once it happened a million times. People loved him."

Chad already knew that, of course; he'd first experienced "Dave's world" during journeyman training at the IMB Missionary Learning Center.

THROUGH DAVE'S WACKY ADVENTURES AND ALL THE CRAZY STUFF HE'D DONE, GOD HAD BEEN PREPARING HIM FOR A DANGEROUS PART OF THE WORLD.

"I remember moving in, meeting him, and thinking, 'Oh, Lord, what have You gotten me into?'" Chad recalls with a laugh. In time, though, Dave became "the brother I never had. We had different personalities and we got on each other's nerves, but we had that brotherhood in Christ that is stronger than blood."

During the next two years, the dynamic duo traveled together from the western edge of North Africa to the Red Sea in the east, from Khartoum, Sudan, in the south to the Mediterranean in the north. They searched out opportunities to reach the unreached, made friends, paved the way for follow-up work. Later, they trained new RASER teams to do the same.

On one unforgettable 10-day trip Dave recounted, they endured

130-degree heat in the daytime; slept outside during a dust storm that whipped up winds to 70 miles an hour; drove 340 kilometers across the desert (twice) in a truck with no air conditioning, a bad radiator and worse battery, a worn fanbelt and a broken door; crossed the Nile four times; eluded a desert cat that invaded their camp; climbed a 500-foot rock cliff; met "tons of very warm, caring and generous people, made several new friends, and shared the good news about (Jesus Christ) with these new friends (a couple of them had NEVER heard of Him before)."

Some of the places they explored were afflicted with extreme poverty, haunted by years of civil war and ethnic conflict, oppressed by militant Islamic rule and persecution of Christians.

"THERE'S NO QUESTION WE WERE THE FIRST CHRISTIANS TO COME INTO CONTACT WITH SOME OF THESE PEOPLE."

"Our job was to go in, travel throughout the country, find out what people groups were located where, and if there were any Christians or churches there," Chad says. "We did the best we could with our limited Arabic to try to give our testimony. Dave was good at it. He picked up the language better than I did. Neither of us really saw any converts, but we were able to share quite a bit. There's no question we were the first Christians to come into contact with some of these people."

But they weren't the last. Long-term work was begun in key

places because of the contacts Dave, Chad, and their RASER teams made. Those contacts are still paying off today.

They were directly involved in the beginning of a church-planting effort that had produced more than 150 congregations by 2004, with many more in development. Fourteen thousand new believers had been baptized. About 250 local leaders had been trained to continue the work. Some had been arrested, tortured, or threatened, but they refused to stop sharing the good news.

"Dave, Chad—I had about 10 journeymen who were all the cream of the crop, and they just blew the area open," Eddie reports. "These guys were totally doing the job. I could turn my back and not even worry. God had sculpted Dave with all the tools he needed. He never said no. Once you asked him to do something, he was going to get it done."

That didn't mean everything went according to plan.

With Dave, something unexpected was bound to occur. It became a joke on the team: If you want to go on a trip you won't forget, go with Dave. The truck will break down. Or you'll get lost. Or you'll eat some really weird food and get sick. But you might just find a village open to the gospel or share Jesus with someone who will change the spiritual history of his whole people group.

"I wasn't so much his supervisor as a guy who hung on for the ride," Eddie admits. "We had other guys who were just as adventurous, but it was like some kind of divine marker followed Dave. Something was going to happen."

He was arrested and questioned in one country while surveying the region to prepare for a volunteer group. He was detained by secret police in another country while distributing the *JESUS* film. Once, while searching for a village on no map, Dave and Chad were held for hours by men waving AK-47s.

Dave loved everything about North Africa—the people, the cultures, the hospitality (most of the time), the craggy landscapes that seemed to stretch to infinity. After more than two years there, his devotion to the region had stretched far beyond the affection of a friendly adventurer. He had begun to love Arabs with a deep, mature, and holy passion—and he wanted to tell them about the God who had given him that love.

If not him, who?

"We'd always talk about that: 'What chance does Abdul—or whoever—have to hear the gospel today?'" Eddie remembers. "If Dave didn't tell him, he didn't have a chance. Dave just couldn't figure out how you could sit in America while people didn't have a chance to hear."

ENCOUNTER IN BETHLEHEM

A year into his assignment, Dave and other journeymen from throughout the region joined thousands of pilgrims in Bethlehem on December 31, 1999, to observe the turn of the millennium at the Church of the Nativity. That night, he met another journeyman named Carrie Taylor. A vivacious blonde from Texas, she was ministering to Arab women and children in the region.

No romantic sparks flew that first evening. "We really didn't pay any attention to each other," Carrie reports.

Afterward, she didn't even remember his name. She later called him "Nathan" while talking to a friend, who corrected her mistake. "Oh well, I'll never see him again," she answered.

But she did see him again—about six months later at a basketball game in which several visiting journeymen were participating. The next day the group went snorkeling in the Red Sea.

"We talked and kind of hit it off," Carrie recalls. "I was comfortable around him. He made me laugh."

THAT NIGHT, HE MET ANOTHER JOURNEYMAN NAMED CARRIE TAYLOR. A VIVACIOUS BLONDE FROM TEXAS, SHE WAS MINISTERING TO ARAB WOMEN AND CHILDREN IN THE REGION.

Dating among journeymen on the field is forbidden by IMB policy. In any case it was impractical for Dave and Carrie, who lived and worked in different parts of the region. So they began an "e-mail courtship."

They were amazed at the things they shared in common, particularly key life verses from the Bible—including Matthew 9:36-38, the specific passage God used to call both of them to missions:

"Seeing the people, He felt compassion for them, because they were distressed and dispirited like sheep without a shepherd. Then He said to His disciples, 'The harvest is plentiful, but the workers are few. Therefore beseech the Lord of the harvest to send out workers into His harvest.'"

They felt it was a "God thing," a confirmation that He had made the two for each other. Moreover, they shared a common heart for the Arab world.

"Right away I noticed his passion for God," Carrie says. "We talked about working with Arab and Muslim people and how we both just loved it. I remember thinking, 'God made one perfect for me.'"

"WE TALKED ABOUT WORKING WITH ARAB AND MUSLIM PEOPLE AND HOW WE BOTH JUST LOVED IT. I REMEMBER THINKING, 'GOD MADE ONE PERFECT FOR ME.'"

Nor did Dave's penchant for adventure scare Carrie off. She even served as a translator on one of his two-week projects for volunteers in North Africa.

When they completed their journeyman terms in 2001, Dave and Carrie both entered Southwestern Baptist Theological Seminary in Fort Worth, Texas, with the intention of preparing for long-term missions service in the Arab world.

On Thanksgiving Day of that year, they went to a family gathering. Dave—armed with roses—proposed.

Their wedding came the following June. His friend David Hale, a groomsman on the big day, says Dave was very serious, and a little nervous. It's the only time he remembers Dave showing fear—besides the time in Texas they were in a tornado's path, and the time Dave lost some maps showing the location of landmines in a war-ravaged part of North Africa.

"A wedding, a tornado, and landmines; it's pretty respectable that nothing else scared him besides those three!" his friend testifies.

The newlywed couple headed back to Fort Worth. Carrie worked full time; Dave worked part time and continued seminary studies. Cliff Lea, Dave's student minister from college days in Canyon, had moved to Travis Avenue Baptist Church in Fort Worth, where the McDonnalls were attending. He handled premarital counseling for Dave and Carrie—and quickly recognized they were a perfect match. They loved Christ, loved each other, and loved the lost.

Cliff saw a huge change in the crazy kid he'd met on the A&M campus years before.

> "A WEDDING, A TORNADO, AND LANDMINES;
> IT'S PRETTY RESPECTABLE THAT NOTHING
> ELSE SCARED HIM BESIDES THOSE THREE!"

"Dave grew in the Lord so fast. He went from being a good ol' boy to being really mature, and missions is what drove him," Cliff observes. "I saw in him one of the most passionate longings for the unreached to know Christ that I have ever witnessed. Here I was his mentor, but he was challenging me. We were doing a lot at Travis Avenue to impact the community, but Dave kept asking, 'What about the nations?' And he was right. He became someone I looked to for my own spiritual gauge."

Dave threw himself into worship with the same passionate abandon he brought to everything else in his life. Cliff will always remember times of worship with a hundred or more seminary students in the Travis Avenue church basement. Dave would be right down front, eyes closed, face lifted to heaven, singing to the Lord in his loud, off-key voice.

In the spring of 2003, American, British, and other coalition forces overthrew Saddam Hussein's long-ruling regime in Iraq. The "hot" part of the war ended in a few months, as Iraqi military forces collapsed in the face of overwhelming coalition firepower.

The Iraqi people, however, faced a long, painful road to recovery from the war, previous conflicts—and the untold devastation wrought by Saddam's generation of abuse. Hunger, poverty, and the lack of clean water and other basics permeated the country, along with continuing violence.

Despite the dangers, secular and religious humanitarian groups moved to respond—including Southern Baptists' overseas relief and development operation. Southern Baptist churches packed and sent thousands of boxes of food for distribution around the country. Relief workers and volunteers delivered the food to needy families, made friends, and looked for ways to assist in long-term development.

In June of that year, a team of 18 Southern Baptist relief volunteers headed into Iraq. Team leaders: Dave and Carrie, who brought their experience in the region and Arabic language skills to the task.

"We both were at a place where we wanted to be on the field more than anything, because that's where our heart was," Carrie says.

When they returned to Texas, though, they had no immediate expectation of returning to Iraq. In a year or two, God willing, they hoped to return to work somewhere in the Arabic-speaking world they had served as journeymen.

But in the early fall, an unexpected and urgent call came from Iraq: Would they consider returning, as soon as possible, to help coordinate humanitarian projects in the north for a year? An answer was needed almost immediately.

Dave and Carrie decided to take 24 hours to pray, fast, and seek God—separately—then come together and discuss what He had revealed.

BUT IN THE EARLY FALL, AN UNEXPECTED AND URGENT CALL CAME FROM IRAQ: WOULD THEY CONSIDER RETURNING, AS SOON AS POSSIBLE.

Dave, who had been studying the Gospel of Luke, dwelled on the story of the rich young ruler in Chapter 18. Jesus confronted the earnest seeker: "One thing you still lack; sell all that you possess, and distribute it to the poor, and you shall have treasure in heaven; and come, follow Me" (verse 22). The young man sadly walked away; he couldn't bring himself to make such a sacrifice.

"For David, that was it," Carrie says. "We were called to give everything and to go."

Meanwhile, in her solitary time with God, Carrie came to John 6:1-14. A young boy gives his paltry meal of five loaves and two fish. Jesus blesses the food and distributes it to 5,000 hungry pilgrims. There is enough for all, and much left over.

"Just give what you have and God will use it," Carrie says of the guidance she received from the Lord.

When she rejoined Dave, "We just prayed there and committed ourselves then. We struggled with it afterward, but it was such a strong calling. It was such a neat thing in our relationship that God basically shared the same thing with each of us, but individually, so that it was more powerful to us."

Dave rushed to finish his classes early as the couple made arrangements for departure. By November 2003, they were back in Iraq.

They immediately plunged into relief work, helping direct the numerous volunteer groups still coming into Iraq. They distributed food to Kurds, to Arabs, to people who had lost their homes and were living in refugee camps. Iraqis were always surprised and delighted by their skill in speaking Arabic.

"You go into a place that is so dark and that just does not have hope, and you offer hope because you have the love of Christ in you," Carrie explains. "People see that. They ask, 'Why do you do this?' We tell them, 'I love the Iraqi people, because Christ loves me.'"

Amid the challenges of the work, they experienced many moments of divine encouragement from God. "We simply clung to Him," says Carrie. "We spent a lot of time in prayer and in His Word, both individually and together."

They also found time to nurture their growing relationship.

"They were pals; they did things together," says a co-worker. "They shared the ups and the downs and the frustrations if things didn't work out."

Carrie, always a good sport, became a skilled "straight man" for Dave's ever-present jokes and stories, enabling him to reach into his bag of comedy routines to lighten the load on workers and volunteers.

"He had a repertoire of stories, and they all had their own little titles," she says. "He liked for me to set him up. If we were in a group that hadn't heard a certain story, I'd say something like, 'You know, one time David was doing so and so. Tell 'em about it, David.' He'd jump on that like a dog on a bone."

Dave, meanwhile, worked hard at being a sensitive husband—a challenge for most young guys new to the marriage relationship. Art and Dottie D., an older Southern Baptist couple who lived and worked with the McDonnalls in Iraq, observed the little things Dave did to express his love for his bride. He managed to sneak in a special Christmas gift for her in their luggage, for example, and keep it hidden until Christmas Day. He looked for ways to make the harsh demands of Iraq easier on her.

"Carrie wasn't a morning person, so David would get up and take his shower and all that, then go back and wake her up so she could sleep a little longer," Dottie confides. "He wouldn't talk to her at the breakfast table for a while until she woke up. I'm married to a 'not morning person' too, so I know how it is."

Carrie confirms the observation with a laugh.

"Dave actually had to learn that the hard way the first few weeks of our marriage," she says. "He didn't even drink coffee, but he learned how to start a pot for me. He was just so giving. He wanted to do as much as he could to help anybody out."

MARCH 15

Trying to help: That's what Dave was doing on March 15, 2004.

Dave and Carrie, joined by Southern Baptist workers Karen Watson and Larry and Jean Elliott, had been investigating human needs in northern Iraq for more than a week. Karen had been serving in and around Iraq for about a year. Larry and Jean, veteran workers in Honduras, had only recently arrived. Larry was an expert in relief work—particularly drilling water wells—and had assisted in several short-term projects in southern Iraq in 2003.

The team had spent days assessing possible water purification projects. They were eager to find places where Iraqis needed clean water. Mosul, Iraq's third-largest city and a violent former stronghold of Saddam Hussein's Baath Party, was such a place.

THEY WERE DRIVING IN THE AREA WHEN, WITHOUT WARNING, ATTACKERS IN ANOTHER VEHICLE PULLED ALONGSIDE AND FIRED AUTOMATIC WEAPONS INTO THEIR TRUCK.

The people they visited March 15 were friendly and receptive— and they desperately needed water. The team members made plans to return.

"We had a great day with them," Carrie says. "They were so eager for our help."

They were driving in the area when, without warning, attackers in another vehicle pulled alongside and fired automatic weapons into their truck—riddling it with bullets, shattering all the windows. All five Southern Baptist workers were hit. Larry, Jean, and Karen died at the scene. Carrie and David, both shot multiple times, survived the initial attack.

At first, David's chances of survival seemed better than Carrie's. He managed to call a co-worker to alert other colleagues and family members.

Three Iraqi men helped move Carrie's broken body from the truck and put her in a taxi, which raced her and David to a local hospital. Normally, Muslim men would never touch any woman not in their family, but these men "treated me like a sister," Carrie says.

"David's thoughts and actions were focused on me," Carrie remembers of those first moments after the attack. "He's the one that got help to remove me from the truck. He's the one that got medical attention for me. He denied his own wounds. He was just taking care of me."

"I love you," she told him.

"I love you, too," he replied.

Carrie closed her eyes, believing she would see David again when she opened them. Doctors put her into a drug-induced coma in preparation for medical evacuation out of Iraq. She would not wake up for eight days.

When she opened her eyes again, Carrie was back in Texas, at Parkland Memorial Hospital in Dallas.

SHE BEGAN ASKING FOR DAVID ALMOST AS SOON AS SHE REGAINED CONSCIOUSNESS.

She had already been through several surgeries while unconscious—and faced several more on the long road to recovery. It would be months before she walked again.

She began asking for David almost as soon as she regained consciousness. Family members put her off, urging her to rest. Finally, she was told he had died in Iraq in the hours after the attack.

What had come before seemed easy compared to the pain that

followed for Carrie, David's family, and many friends. For all who had experienced his love, his passion for God and for the lost, his sheer joy in living, the sudden silence that replaced his laughter seemed too much to bear.

As the weeks passed, however, and her remarkable physical recovery progressed, Carrie's spiritual strength began to shine through. From her wheelchair, or gripping a walker or a cane, she began to reassure grieving friends—and exhort churches not to back from their global task in a dangerous world. Three months after the attack, she spoke at the 2004 Southern Baptist Convention meeting in Indianapolis. She acknowledged her body and her heart were broken, but that God remained sovereign and full of love.

"We have to keep going to the hard places. We have to keep going to the violent places," Carrie challenged listeners. "God's call was not just to go to places that are easy.

"I hope this fires people up, not that they say, 'I can't go. Look at her, look at the tragedy in her life,' but rather say, 'Look how God has overcome this.' He will be glorified to the uttermost parts of the world, and the church needs to rise up and go."

Her determination has grown only stronger in the days since.

She expects to be challenged by those—including many Christians—who believe David paid far too high a price. Live and let live, some say: If people don't want us over there, bring the missionaries home. The world is too risky these days to keep sending our best and brightest.

"I'm sure one of these days, when I'm not limping and the scars aren't quite as red, somebody will say that to my face," she acknowledges. "I expect it from the world, but when believers say it, it breaks my heart. They need to go back and review what Jesus did. They need to look at their Bible, because God does not lead us to an easy life. He said, 'If the world treated Me this way, it's going to treat you this way.'"

DAVE'S LEGACY

What legacy does David McDonnall leave behind?

A legacy of joy and laughter, of love and servanthood, of deep friendship and "brotherhood stronger than blood," as his North Africa partner Chad B. says.

"If I could have stepped in front of that bullet for him, I would have," Chad states without hesitation.

"DAVID WAS LESS AFRAID OF DYING THAN HE WAS OF NOT LIVING HIS LIFE. AND THE LIFE HE LIVED WAS THE LIFE OF CHRIST."

"My children's children will tell stories about Dave," adds David Hale. "Since March 15 my life has changed. I am no longer simply a Christian. I want to be a man who gives my life totally to God. After Dave gave his life, the least we can do is completely give our life to Christ."

Donna McDonnall misses her son more than anyone who hasn't lost a child can ever imagine. But she knows he lived his life believing he was fulfilling God's purpose for his life.

"David was less afraid of dying than he was of not living his life," she says. "And the life he lived was the life of Christ."

Life in Christ: That is David's primary legacy.

"The love of God and the power of Christ can change any heart," he once said. God "can turn people from violence into carrying the Sword of the Spirit … and piercing the hearts of people, not with bullets, but with the Word of God."

Dave had an overpowering life wish—and an overpowering passion to share it with the people who needed it most.

Was it worth the risk? Is it worth the risk of your own life—or your children's lives? You decide.

LARRY AND JEAN ELLIOTT

living water, pure love

Larry & 6 *Jean Elliott*

No, no, no.

It can't be true. Please, dear God, don't let it be true.

Such was the anguished reaction from hundreds of friends, colleagues and family members of Larry and Jean Elliott when the news began to spread on that terrible day of March 15, 2004:

After only 23 days in Iraq, Larry and Jean had been shot by anonymous gunmen while driving on a highway near the city of Mosul. The Elliotts and a Southern Baptist co-worker had died instantly in the attack. Two others were critically wounded; one of them also would die.

How could it happen? How could the Elliotts' service to so many, for so long, be cut off with such sudden cruelty? How could life go on without Larry's room-shaking laugh, Jean's gentle smile— and the commitment, the love, the sheer joy they brought to each day and relationship?

LARRY'S UNVARNISHED RESPONSE: "YES, WE COULD GET KILLED."

Family and church friends in North Carolina had concerns about the Iraq assignment—and had expressed them to Larry and Jean— months before the veteran missionary couple left for the region.

Larry's unvarnished response: "Yes, we could get killed."

But he repeatedly reminded everyone of the Apostle Paul's words about a believer's mortality: "Absent from the body, present with the Lord." He and Jean expressed a strong sense of God's call to the hurting people of a broken land—and strong confidence in God's provision.

Their reassurances provided a measure of comfort to those left behind in the dark days after their deaths. But the pain still cut knife-deep in the hearts of their children, their brothers and sisters, their countless friends in multiple countries.

Larry and Jean's love was so deep, their friendship so faithful, that its absence was unthinkable. In Honduras, where they were adored by throngs of people whose lives they had touched during a quarter-century of missionary service, the grief was almost unbearable.

"Why did they have to go?" sobbed Maria, the Elliotts' long-time housekeeper and close friend, when told of the attack. "Why did they have to go? I told them it was going to be too dangerous!"

For some Hondurans, despair over losing their dear friends mixed with anger. Several Baptist pastors nurtured by Larry through the years told International Mission Board officials their friend and mentor never should have been allowed to go to Iraq.

Some old friends back home in North Carolina who heard the tragic news weren't even aware that the Elliotts had begun working in Iraq.

Surely it was some kind of mistake, thought Marion D. Lark, retired pastor of First Baptist Church of Henderson, North Carolina. He'd been a fan of Larry and Jean since First Baptist provided a house during two missionary furloughs the family took in the 1980s.

"I thought the Elliotts were safe in Honduras," Lark wrote soon after the incident. "Unknown to me, they had been in Iraq since February on a humanitarian mission to help provide fresh water."

However, he added, "I'm not in the least surprised to learn they went where the need was great for the service they could render."

After recovering from the initial shock of loss, others reached the same conclusion. Even if they had known the violent fate that awaited them in Iraq, several family members acknowledged, Larry and Jean probably would have gone anyway.

Charlotte Observer columnist Joe DePriest, a friend of Jean's from high school days, admitted to having a harder time under-standing the Elliotts' radical move. He had written about them for the local newspaper in Shelby, N.C., many years before. They gave up a nice house—and Larry left a good job—to move to Honduras, one of the poorest countries in the Western Hemisphere. When DePriest asked why they were going, their reply echoed other mis-sionaries he had interviewed: "They had a call, and they couldn't run from it."

But that was long ago. Why go to Iraq, amid the deadly chaos of terrorism, in the twilight of a long and fruitful ministry?

"Missionary zeal is one thing," DePriest wrote. "But Larry, 60, and Jean, 58, had two sons, a daughter, and nine grandchildren. From all reports they were doing good work in Central America. They could even have retired. Why, at their age, did they put them-selves in the middle of a shooting war?"

They were good people who wanted to help others, he concluded.

But that doesn't adequately explain the Elliotts' decision, which seems irrational to many reasonable people. God's logic follows His paths—not our limited, fearful pace. He calls us to trust and obey, whether or not we understand. If we say yes, He gives us peace beyond understanding.

Larry and Jean "spent their whole lives saying yes to Him," observes their daughter, Gina Kim. "And seeing where He led them, I can't argue with God."

SOMETHING DIFFERENT

In his mind's eye, Joe DePriest still sees the giggling, fun-loving Jean of 40 years ago, the girl who sat in the desk in front of him in geometry class at Shelby High School. They talked before, after —and during—class about the latest hit songs, how to dance "The Twist" and "who was dating whom."

Yet even then, Jean was something special. Her smile wasn't reserved just for friends or popular kids. When a new student, Myrna Hoyle, arrived at Shelby High, she stood alone, self-conscious and lonely in line at the cafeteria on her first day in school.

"I understand you're the new girl," said a friendly voice behind her. "I'm Jean. The grilled cheese sandwich here won't kill you. It's very good, really."

A fast friendship formed that day. Jean took Myrna under her wing and introduced her to others. "I saw her do that for other people, too," Myrna told DePriest. "She was kind of a missionary back then."

Even in those early days, Myrna says, Jean seemed to have a special "radar" that zeroed in on people who needed a kind word, a hug, a friend.

Jean was born September 21, 1945, in Shelby, the seventh of

eight children of Robert and Irene Dover. The Dovers lived in the mill village in Shelby, where most folks had to scrabble hard for a living. Both parents worked at the textile mill to feed their large family, but Mrs. Dover found time to teach her children about the Lord—and take them to His house.

"Second Baptist Church in Shelby was a vital part of my life," Jean wrote of her early years. "I have always attended church since infancy. The first Christian influence on my life was my mother, who realized the importance of being in God's house and worshiping. She would talk with our family about the Bible, using sayings from Proverbs and other Scripture in leading us. Her beliefs were synonymous with her life. I am grateful to God for being blessed with a Christian mother."

"THERE WAS SOMETHING DIFFERENT ABOUT JEAN. SHE ALWAYS WANTED TO BE A MISSIONARY, EVEN WHEN SHE WAS A LITTLE GIRL."

During a spring revival in 1955 at Second Baptist, 9-year-old Jean asked Jesus Christ to be her Savior. She participated in all the children's, youth, and choir programs at church, including the mission groups—and became a leader in most of them. When she reached 16, she started working part time (full time in the summers) as a salesclerk at Wray's Department Store.

In her later childhood and youth, Jean spent at least as much time with her oldest sister, Nanci, who had married Buford Ellis, as she did at home.

"I was 10 years older than Jean, and when we got married, we feel like we raised her," Nanci remembers. "She was at our house all the time and she went everywhere we went. She was always a special child. There was something different about Jean. She always wanted to be a missionary, even when she was a little girl."

Folks at Second Baptist helped instill that desire and nurtured it through the years. When she finished high school in 1963, Jean entered Appalachian State Teachers College in Boone, North Carolina, to study elementary education.

Meanwhile, a country boy named Larry Elliott—born October 12, 1943—was growing up on his family's tobacco farm in Grassy Creek, a bucolic stretch in rural Granville County near the North Carolina/Virginia border. His parents, Conway and Lelia Elliott, raised Larry to do what most farm kids do: work.

"My earliest childhood memories are of my brother and me playing as we did chores on the farm," Larry said of those days. When school was in session, they walked a country mile to meet the bus, walked a mile home. But that didn't mean escape from farm chores:

"As spring would come, the afternoons were spent plowing and planting. Even though there were only a couple hours of daylight left after we came home from school, we were expected to pitch in and help wherever we were needed."

Pitching in and helping—that's a habit Larry practiced for a lifetime.

But work didn't keep Larry away from church. Like Jean, he felt "a strange stirring" at age 9 during revival services at Grassy Creek Baptist Church. Convinced he was a sinner, he went with his mother after the service to talk to the preacher. On a hot, humid July evening, he asked Jesus Christ to be his Lord and Savior. He grew in the

Lord, and twice during high school served as Youth Sunday preacher.

"People seemed to expect me to become a preacher. But I didn't think God wanted me behind the pulpit," he said.

> "PEOPLE SEEMED TO EXPECT ME TO BECOME A PREACHER. BUT I DIDN'T THINK GOD WANTED ME BEHIND THE PULPIT."

Wake Forest University wanted Larry, a good athlete, on the basketball court. The school offered him a full scholarship, but he wanted to study textile technology, a program Wake Forest didn't have. He graduated first in his class in high school and was awarded a textile scholarship by North Carolina State University.

Textile engineering, Larry said, offered "the opportunity to design something and make it, and I wanted that."

Between his sophomore and junior years, Larry spent the summer working as a technician at Pittsburgh Plate Glass Company in Shelby. It was good experience, but God steered him to Shelby for a more important reason.

"That summer I also met Jean Dover, who was everything I ever wanted in a girl," he later wrote. "The next summer we were married. My senior year at State was one of the best years of my life. My grades improved, and although we had very little money, we enjoyed just being together."

Their first son, Scott, was born in 1966, the year Larry finished college. He worked for a time as production foreman with National Plastics in Maryland, where Jean taught elementary school. U.S. Army service summoned Larry, and the young family spent 21 months in Germany, where second son Todd was born in 1968. At a Baptist church in Germany, pastor Ray Reynolds and his wife, Helen (who later became Southern Baptist missionaries), helped the Elliotts grow spiritually in many ways. Larry now felt the Lord calling him to preach, to which he wholeheartedly responded.

"The inner peace I felt from that surrender has become a standard by which I have measured other spiritual commitments," he reflected.

A tough and lonely hitch in Vietnam had to come first, however. While Larry was gone, Jean saw a movie about legendary missionary Lottie Moon during the 1969 Week of Prayer for Foreign Missions. Her childhood attraction to missions resurfaced in a powerful way. But as a young mother with two children, another baby on the way, and a husband off at war, she didn't know how to react.

"I felt God speaking to me," she said. "But I wasn't sure what was happening. I wrote to Larry and shared with him what I had felt, and thought that was the end of it."

It wasn't.

When Larry came home in mid-1970, he held 4-month-old daughter Gina for the first time. He also landed a good job as quality control manager with Macfield Texturing in Reidsville, North Carolina. There he and Jean settled down and became active members of a congregation they would cherish for the rest of their lives: Baptist Temple Church. They served and ministered in many ways, and their sense of call to full-time ministry continued to deepen. Jean heard a missionary couple share their experiences at a local gathering and felt a strong stirring within once again. She and Larry knelt in their den and asked God to reveal His direction.

On June 7, 1975, Larry clearly heard God calling him overseas—to preach behind the Iron Curtain, he thought at the time. The next day, he stopped his car on the side of the road and bowed his head to pray.

"I surrendered," he said. "I knew I had to resign my job and enter seminary."

> THE NEXT DAY, HE STOPPED HIS CAR ON THE SIDE OF THE ROAD AND BOWED HIS HEAD TO PRAY. "I SURRENDERED. I KNEW I HAD TO RESIGN MY JOB AND ENTER SEMINARY."

He did just that, with Jean's enthusiastic support, and earned a master of divinity degree with an emphasis in Christian counseling at Southeastern Baptist Theological Seminary in Wake Forest. While studying, he served for a year as pastor of Wakeminster Baptist Church in Raleigh. Jean finished her undergraduate studies at Meredith College in Raleigh and completed the seminary courses required for appointment by the Foreign (now International) Mission Board.

GOD'S HAND

In June of 1978, Larry and Jean became Southern Baptist missionaries.

That was long before the end of the Soviet Union, however. There were no calls for North Carolina preacher boys behind the Iron Curtain. There was, however, an opening for a chaplain with counseling skills at a government hospital served by Southern Baptist missionaries in Tegucigalpa, capital of the Central American nation of Honduras. Larry and Jean were ready and willing to go.

Missionary Carl Rees remembers the first time he met the excited North Carolina couple early in 1978. Carl and his wife, Martha, also were candidates for missionary service in Honduras. They joined other prospective workers for meetings with personnel consultants at the Foreign Mission Board in Richmond, Virginia.

"We were getting ready to take a break and this couple walked over," Carl recalls. "Larry said, 'You're Carl and Martha, right? Well, we're Larry and Jean and we're going to Honduras, too.' We became instant friends. Every time we had a chance to sit together to eat or visit, we did it. That's the kind of people they were."

The two couples went through the rest of the interview process together, were appointed together, trained as new missionaries together, studied Spanish in Costa Rica together, flew to Honduras for the first time together. From Larry's jokes about the dreaded medical exams required of missionary candidates to Jean's heartfelt prayers for any and every need, the long months of preparation for service were made easier by going through them with the Elliotts.

It was the same in Honduras, where they grew ever closer through good times and bad. Carl enjoyed watching the vibrant couple attract others like human magnets. They treated everyone— missionaries or Hondurans, powerful officials or poor villagers—the same way.

"Larry was a big guy (6-foot-2 and 250 pounds), and big guys are an attraction in a society where most of the people are small,"

Carl explains. "And he just never met a stranger. I don't think it ever entered his mind to ignore somebody, to not include them. If you ever heard his laugh, it just warmed everything."

> "I DON'T THINK IT EVER ENTERED HIS MIND TO IGNORE SOMEBODY, TO NOT INCLUDE THEM. IF YOU EVER HEARD HIS LAUGH, IT JUST WARMED EVERYTHING."

And you could hear his laugh—which became known all over Honduras—a long way off.

"Larry was easily recognizable from a distance," says missionary Peggy Johnson. "A tall man who towered over most Hondurans, you could easily spot his Southern swagger and broad-brimmed hat. He was always surrounded by people. Once you drew closer, you were immediately taken with his cheerful Carolina drawl and loud, infectious laugh that left you laughing along with him—even if you had no idea what was so funny."

Missionary Joyce Harms, another close friend of the Elliotts from the beginning, was sitting in a packed, pitch-dark movie theater in Tegucigalpa one day when she heard a familiar guffaw.

"Larry?" she called out.

"Joyce?" came the reply. Sure enough, it was Larry.

Jean, on the other hand, wasn't loud at all. But she was just as welcoming—maybe more so—in her gentle way. Her smile, her spirit, somehow "instantly communicated kindness" to everyone she encountered, Peggy says. Women, children, families flocked to her house or her arms for the "Jean treatment."

Popular as they were, however, the Elliotts faced a career-threatening crisis almost as soon as they reached Honduras: Larry no longer had a job. The government had changed between their missionary appointment and their arrival in the country. Chances for filling the chaplain post at the government hospital had rapidly narrowed from slim to none. Larry and Jean experienced some anxious months wondering and praying about what God might be up to.

"Larry really felt a call to work one-on-one with people in need, and he thought that was going to be in the area of counseling and chaplaincy," Carl Rees says. "So he didn't know what he would do. But he knew that God had called him to Honduras. As you look back on it, you can see God's hand in it."

God's hand was guiding Larry's skillful hands, his creative mind—and his open heart, which went out to the poor he saw all around him.

"Part of my calling is to work with my hands in sharing some of the talents God has given me," Larry wrote. Those talents included his engineering and design abilities, as well as the down-home ingenuity he learned growing up on a farm.

WHATEVER IT TAKES

Honduras is a desperately poor country. Malnutrition, lack of basic hygiene in rural villages, widespread lack of access to clean water and basic medical care—all handicap or kill countless Hondurans. Floods, drought, and periodic epidemics increase the suffering.

As the Elliotts were searching for God's place for them in missionary ministry in the late '70s and early '80s, Honduran Baptists were becoming increasingly active in social ministries. Meeting physical needs, they recognized, was a tangible way to demonstrate the love of Jesus Christ and extend the gospel. Veteran Southern Baptist missionaries like evangelist Harold Hurst, nurse practitioner Frances Crawford, and physician David Harms were already using rural medical and dental clinics and other community ministries—bolstered by Southern Baptist volunteers—to till new fields for planting churches.

Larry began to see all kinds of possibilities for meeting human needs, aiding communities, and "earning the right" to share the gospel. The Elliotts and their missionary colleagues realized he was the man to coordinate the mission's relief and social ministries.

"He was a practical, hands-on guy, with a deep heart of love," recalls Harms, a close friend and colleague from the beginning. "The needs in Honduras are so overwhelming, and Larry was able to plug in because of his outgoing personality and his ability to relate to Hondurans."

His first long-term foray into social ministry was the "El Coco Project."

Larry mobilized missionaries, Honduran Baptists, medical volunteers, and the Honduran government's health department to bring latrines, medical care, and water to the rural community of El Coco in 1980. When the project began, the village of nearly 200 homes lacked a single usable latrine. Villagers hauled water from a polluted river, where they also washed. Nearly every child suffered from multiple internal parasites. The Baptists held medical and dental clinics, treated hundreds of patients, helped build latrines, taught basic hygiene, and held evangelistic services nightly.

"The emphasis was physical health during the day and spiritual health in the evenings," the Elliotts wrote in a 1980 newsletter. "Jesus ministered to both areas and He calls us to do the same. As a result of this effort, we saw the government health promoter, who was sent to the village to supervise the project, accept Jesus Christ as Savior— along with many other men who had not experienced a personal relationship with our Lord. An influential cantina owner accepted Christ and has stopped selling alcoholic drinks in his cantina. Pray for these new Christians. ..."

The ongoing project later helped provide potable water for all of the community's 1,500 people.

Larry's direction was set. He began to pioneer a variety of relief and development ministries in isolated, hungry, or disaster-prone areas throughout Honduras.

"Natural disasters are a part of life in Honduras," Carl Rees says. "If it's not flooding, it's drought. People lose their crops by one or the other—often by both. Larry was always involved in feeding kinds of ministries, whether it was seed for corn or disaster relief."

Food-for-work projects became a regular part of Larry's tool bag, enabling hungry villagers to build (or rebuild) their communities while feeding their families. Farming cooperatives and vocational training became other tools. Larry and his long-time social ministry partner, missionary Jim Palmer, spearheaded the launch of a vocational training center in Tegucigalpa in the late '80s to help pastors, their wives, and other Hondurans learn carpentry, sewing, and other marketable skills.

Larry analyzed problems, found answers. He studied geology, agriculture, parasitology—anything it took to help local people overcome suffering and become self-sufficient. Then he turned the programs he designed over to them.

When he saw how much a big truck could help with delivery of supplies, building materials, and food to various projects, church friends in the United States donated a used dump truck. In an epic

> "WHATEVER IT TAKES—LARRY WAS ONTO THAT LONG BEFORE IT BECAME A BUZZWORD IN MISSIONS."

12-day journey, Larry drove it all the way to Honduras through Mexico and the Central American peninsula. He found plenty of other uses for the truck, too—like hauling kids from miles around to Sunday School at his latest church start.

"Whatever it takes—Larry was onto that long before it became a buzzword in missions," explains David Harms. "There was one community, Alubaren, that desperately needed some development projects with a road and a church. I went out there to see how things were going and found Larry with the dump truck down in a ditch, lying on his back in the mud fixing it. We got it out and got it going again. This was a very depressed area, and the crops had failed; some years the rain comes and some years it doesn't. Larry set up a food-for-work program and they worked on different community projects the mayor wanted. They would be paid in corn, beans, and oil so they could eat and feed their families."

Before the project, one local Baptist pastor had been going to bed hungry: He was ashamed to eat when his people had no food. When the project got going, 40-man teams worked in shifts digging trenches for a potable water system. Evangelistic outreach in the area took off.

"A revival has broken out," Larry reported in 1985. "People like never before are accepting Christ as Lord and Savior."

Local folks knew somebody cared about them and their neglected town—Larry. If God had sent this man, they reasoned, He must care about us, too.

It was like that in many places. Practical assistance opened the spiritual door.

"Larry was a make-it-happen guy, a solutions guy," Harms observes. "He would come up with a solution. At first you would think it was harebrained, and he'd sit there and think a little bit more. And all of a sudden you would buy into it. The solution had to fit the problem in a unique way. Whatever a community needed, whether it was urban or rural, he could help. He probably knew more of the geography of Honduras than anybody else I know. He had been everywhere in the country and knew the idiosyncrasies of the different communities."

As time went on, however, Larry realized one solution was overwhelmingly needed in most places: clean water.

"Since gastrointestinal illness is the number one cause of death in Honduras, and most areas in Honduras have unsafe drinking water, helping churches get a potable water source is a high priority,"

Larry stressed. And if churches helped provide clean water to their communities, the people would be far more likely to open their hearts to the Living Water of Christ.

Beginning with little detailed knowledge of water and well-drilling technology, Larry eventually became an expert on the subject. Using a small, donated well-drilling rig, he brought clean drinking water to dozens of towns and villages. He also developed a wide network of churches in the United States that sent hundreds of volunteers to help in aid projects and share the gospel.

Buford and Nanci Ellis (Jean's sister) were two of the Elliotts' most enthusiastic volunteers.

"We made about 15 trips there," Buford recalls. "People loved to work with them. If you ever went once, you'd go back again."

> "WE PUT THE PUMP IN, HOOKED IT UP, AND GOT THEM WATER RUNNING. I TELL YOU, WHEN THOSE HONDURANS SAW WATER RUNNING ON TOP OF THAT MOUNTAIN, THEY WERE SHOUTING AND PRAISING THE LORD. THAT WAS A SIGHT TO SEE!"

Buford will never forget the people of one Honduran community high atop a mountain. Villagers had to haul water in buckets for an hour up the slopes to meet their daily needs. Larry hired a local team to drill a well, but Buford joined a volunteer group that finished the project. It was dusk, and villagers lined up with water containers in anticipation.

"We put the pump in, hooked it up, and got the water running," Buford says. "I tell you, when those Hondurans saw water running on top of that mountain, they were shouting and praising the Lord. That was a sight to see!"

Before the Elliotts left Honduras, 80 water wells had been dug, 12 Baptist churches started and more than 90 mission points launched through their personal ministry.

UNCONDITIONAL FRIENDSHIP

Jean often accompanied Larry on his frequent excursions around the country. When she stayed behind, she developed her own varied ministry of love. Through the churches they started together, through her home, through simple acts of love, she touched other missionaries, volunteers, Honduran women, children—and countless friends.

"JEAN'S MAIN THING WAS BUILDING RELATIONSHIPS. SHE CARED ABOUT THE PERSON FIRST, AND THEN THE WORK. BUT SHE DIDN'T CONSIDER IT WORK. IT WAS JOY TO HER."

There's no telling how many people considered Jean their best and closest friend; she seemingly had an endless capacity for friendship.

With the many demands of motherhood and ministry, where did she find the time?

"That *was* her ministry," insists missionary Tina Torbert, who was immediately drawn into Jean's circle of love when she arrived in Honduras in 1999. "She took me so many places with her to visit people who dearly loved her. Jean's main thing was building relationships. She cared about the person first, and then the work. But she didn't consider it work. It was joy to her."

Joyce Harms, a friend for 25 years, agrees.

"I don't know that I've ever had a friend like Jean," Joyce reflects. "We shared lots of happiness, lots of sorrow. We shared things about our families and about Hondurans. It got to the place where we were so close for a time that we even dressed alike without knowing it. She would come to pick me up and we'd both have on a pink or a blue blouse!"

Jean's love streamed out in many directions. Teaching English. Discipling Honduran women one-on-one. Opening her home to any number of people. Giving special gifts to friends. Praying, praying, and praying some more. When you asked Jean to pray for you, you could count on being prayed for—not only by Jean, but also by her extensive e-mail prayer network.

Then there were her hugs.

"She was the BEST at giving hugs," Tina says. "A handshake never was enough for Jean."

Like Larry's friendship, Jean's love knew no class distinctions. She often asked Tina to come along when she took a Honduran friend, who was confined to a wheelchair, on special trips to a big mall in the capital. Her friend was poor and probably never would have seen the inside of the mall if Jean hadn't taken her.

Her sister, Nanci, watched Jean in action many times during her frequent visits to Honduras.

"She would go with her chalkboard to a (slum) neighborhood

where these three ladies lived in a house with a dirt floor," Nanci recalls. "She taught them to read and write, and they would just talk and talk. She loved to teach. She would teach ladies how to bake and decorate cakes. She had shoeboxes full of donated eyeglasses. People would come to her house and she would fit them with glasses, and they would cry and praise the Lord because they could read their Bibles. She would fix up gifts of baby supplies and take them to the hospital where the poor mothers had their babies. She stood in line for hours at a time to help people get visas at the embassy. She had so many ministries that I can't name them all."

> "I WILL NEVER FORGET THE SIGHT OF LEDIN PUSHING HIS LITTLE WALKER HURRIEDLY THROUGH THE MUD, ANXIOUS FOR A HUG FROM LARRY AND JEAN."

Jean (and Larry) loved children—and helped hundreds of them in small and large ways. North Carolina Baptist editor Tony Cartledge, a friend and admirer, remembers driving in 2002 with the Elliotts along a winding road from Tegucigalpa to Nuevo Sacramento, a fast-growing new community where they were helping a new church.

"There they introduced me to Ledin Rodas, a young boy who was crippled by brittle bone disease," Cartledge writes. "The Elliotts had worked with North Carolina volunteers to facilitate medical treatment that enabled Ledin to achieve his dream of being able to walk.

"I will never forget the sight of Ledin pushing his little walker hurriedly through the mud, anxious for a hug from Larry and Jean."

The Elliotts personally financed innumerable small scholarships to enable Honduran children to attend school, buy textbooks, and obtain school uniforms. Jean often delivered the school supplies herself. Perhaps her proudest achievement: the beginning of a Christian school at one of the churches they started.

She also delighted in enlisting her own three children in mission work. Daughter Gina, now an optometrist, remembers translating at age 12 for volunteers who visited Honduras—including an optometrist who inspired her to pursue that field. As an adult, she often returned to Honduras, not just to visit Mom and Dad but also to serve as a volunteer herself.

"We were definitely involved in their ministry," Gina says. "Wherever they went, we went, unless we were in school. That influenced my life."

As productive as they were in their parallel ministries, Larry and Jean were, first and last, Larry *and* Jean: husband and wife, best friends, missionary partners.

"When I think of the Elliotts as a couple, two things come to mind," writes Peggy Johnson. "First is how much they were loved. From fellow missionaries to Hondurans to (U.S.) supporters, everyone who knew them loved them. Second is how much they loved each other. It's impossible to think of one without the other. They shared not just a home, but a ministry, a life. They even read books together —Jean reading aloud to Larry. … They were always a team."

Carl and Martha Rees remember the difficult days after their son was diagnosed with a malignant tumor during their language school days in Costa Rica.

"A lot of people helped us during that time, but Larry and Jean almost never left our side," Carl says. "They were always there to help, to pray, or whatever. They weren't just the kind of folks you could call any hour of the day or night. You didn't have to call; as soon as they heard about a need, they rushed to see what they could do to meet it. It didn't make any difference if you were a missionary or a Honduran, a church member or not a church member. You were a friend."

The Reeses and many others were able to return that love, ministering to the Elliotts when Jean almost died of malaria—and when Larry faced a bout with cancer in the 1980s. But no one loved the Elliotts quite like they loved others.

It's no wonder so many Hondurans asked the missionary couple to be *padrinos*—honorary official hosts—at weddings, to be present at births, to sit beside deathbeds, to be a part of the family at other joyful or sad moments of life.

"Every time we went somewhere with them, they were well-known—not just as 'missionaries' but as folks who loved others unconditionally," says Tina Torbert. "We stood with them by the bedside of a church member who was dying of AIDS. Larry read Scripture and prayed over Carlos that day. He didn't know us by our names (at that point in his illness), but he knew that we loved him."

CALL TO A THIRSTY LAND

Larry's relief ministry reached a climax in the aftermath of Hurricane Mitch, which devastated huge swaths of Honduras in 1998.

The storm's path of destruction left more than 5,000 Hondurans dead and more than 200,000 homeless. Larry helped lead Honduran Baptists, missionaries, and volunteers in efforts ranging from food deliveries on the backs of mules to stranded villages and the planting of garden plots to road clearing, bridge building, and housing reconstruction.

"He was right in there," says David Harms. "He worked endlessly on food distribution and rebuilding."

Larry also saw God work through the tragedy to open many areas to the gospel. Hundreds of new churches sprang up in the months and years after Mitch.

"We are in the midst of one of the most powerful revivals I have ever experienced," he said at the time.

> "WE ARE IN THE MIDST OF ONE OF THE MOST POWERFUL REVIVALS I HAVE EVER EXPERIENCED."

Larry's innovations in relief and development work, particularly in providing clean water to communities, led the International Mission Board to name him coordinator of disaster relief throughout Middle America and the Caribbean region. He played a key role in responding to a series of hurricanes and other natural disasters in Mexico, El Salvador, Belize, and the Dominican Republic.

"He was full of questions, full of thinking, full of strategic ways we could be involved in disaster relief," says IMB human needs specialist Jim Brown, who brainstormed many projects with Larry. "He would keep me up all hours of the night talking and bouncing ideas off me about how we could be more proactive."

And he turned theory into reality. When he hit the ground,

"Larry could get things done, then remove the American face" and let locals take over, Jim says. "He knew how to meet the needs of people, but also how to share the love of Christ in a very effective way. He knew they went hand in glove; he was not there to do one or the other, but to do both."

For several years, however, Larry and Jean had been praying about the possibility of a more radical change in their ministry assignment—and location. They weren't sure what or where, but they felt the familiar stirring within that had brought them to Honduras long before.

"Larry had come to the idea that maybe his job was finished," says David Harms. "He could go on in Honduras and enjoy a very fruitful, rewarding ministry—and become sort of a patriarch. I don't think they wanted that."

Since his days of wanting to go behind the Iron Curtain, Larry had never lost his desire to go to difficult places with the love of Christ. In the days immediately after the overthrow of Saddam Hussein in Iraq, the Elliotts watched the news and saw images of people struggling to survive amid the chaos. One day, Larry saw a TV report showing elderly Iraqi men dipping buckets in dirty puddles for something to drink.

"I could help them," he told himself.

When the opportunity arose to accompany relief specialist Jim Brown on a trip to southern Iraq soon after coalition invasion, Larry seized it. Donning helmets and flak jackets, the relief team members transported water purification units to several hospitals in the region that once was Ur—Abraham's ancient homeland.

"Before we had been there long at all, Larry just knew God had laid that country on his heart," Jim says. "I had no idea at the time that he was thinking about actually changing his address to Iraq."

> "LARRY JUST KNEW GOD HAD LAID THAT
> COUNTRY ON HIS HEART. I HAD NO IDEA AT
> THE TIME THAT HE WAS THINKING ABOUT
> ACTUALLY CHANGING HIS ADDRESS TO IRAQ."

But he was. He possessed the expertise to organize effective relief and development projects desperately needed in Iraq—particularly water purification. And as he returned home and prayed with Jean, both became convinced that God was calling them to Iraq and her suffering people. Larry went to Iraq without Jean a second time to meet other Christian relief workers and make plans for the big move.

Friends and family members urged them to go someplace— anyplace—else. The Elliotts responded gently, but firmly. At several family gatherings in North Carolina, Larry and Jean shared the opportunities and the risks.

"Yes, we were concerned," admits brother-in-law Buford Ellis. "We talked with them at length, but it wasn't our decision to make. They were perfectly at peace because that's where the Lord wanted them to go."

Long-time friends and supporters at Baptist Temple Church in Reidsville prayed over the kneeling couple before their departure— just as they had before the Elliotts went to Honduras a quarter-century before.

During a Christmas candlelight service at daughter Gina's church, Second Baptist in Houston, Jean explained their call in a way that made it unmistakably clear. At the end of the service, all lights were extinguished except for a single candle, which dimly illuminated the sanctuary.

"This is Iraq," Jean told her daughter, tears rolling down her cheeks. "We're going to a dark place and we're taking the light of Jesus."

IN HIS HANDS

When the Elliotts arrived in Baghdad in late February 2004 after an exhausting 10-hour taxi ride from the Jordanian border, Jean had a notebook in her hand.

"WE'RE GOING TO A DARK PLACE AND WE'RE TAKING THE LIGHT OF JESUS."

"She wanted to know how to say 'Hello' in Arabic," says a former member of the Iraq team. "She couldn't wait to learn some words so she could make friends."

Jean kept her sister Nanci and a host of other prayer partners updated with daily e-mails and instant messages, and her growing excitement was obvious.

"We are happy to be here, and our calling has been confirmed," she declared February 24. A week later: "Little by little we are learning ... It's very different here from any place we have lived, but the people are the same. ... God is so REAL!!! No matter what happens, we are in His hands and know that we are where we should be."

Despite the language barrier, Iraqi women, like Hondurans, were immediately drawn to her warmth, her smile. She embraced the gracious Arab culture of hospitality, drank tea with women who spoke some English, compared notes on grandchildren. With those who spoke only Arabic, she practiced the few words she knew, then

> "WE ARE HAPPY TO BE HERE, AND OUR CALLING HAS BEEN CONFIRMED. NO MATTER WHAT HAPPENS, WE ARE IN HIS HANDS AND KNOW THAT WE ARE WHERE WE SHOULD BE."

tried … Spanish. Carrie McDonnall, who would later survive the attack that killed the Elliotts and her husband, David, heard Jean interacting with some curious Iraqi women one day.

"She was talking to them in Spanish," Carrie reports. "I asked, 'Why are you doing that?' And Jean goes, 'Well, I know that I should be speaking to them in a foreign language, and Spanish is the only one I know!' These Iraqi ladies just ate it up. They were laughing and hugging on her. It was great. I believe Jean's spirit spoke through the language barrier."

Jean and Larry also befriended two children near the guesthouse where they briefly stayed in Baghdad.

"I want to tell you about two little children that Larry and I have grown to love—a sister and a brother, Fatima, 5, and Ali, 4," Jean wrote in an e-mail home. "Every time they see us walking, they come running to hold our hands and walk with us, full of smiles and laughter. They are so cute and take my mind and heart back to Honduras. … The little girl never seems to have her hair combed but she is full of happiness and love. … We did not speak each other's language but we communicated. It's amazing what smiles and laughter can do. … When they got to the corner of the street, they asked us to bend down so they could kiss us, and then they skipped happily back to where their parents were.

"Please pray that we can be a light to these people and that they will come to know the True Light."

With his long experience in relief work, Larry brought a maturity and depth to the mostly young humanitarian team. He knew what needed to be done and how to do it, but he never pulled rank on anyone.

"Larry and Jean made a huge impression on David and me from the moment we heard of their coming to Iraq," says Carrie. "Although they both had way more field experience than we did, they didn't hesitate to ask us about culture or language. They were willing to learn from us 'younguns.' Larry and Jean were servants."

Larry and David, both humorists, enjoyed each other's company. Dave would regale Larry with his repertoire of stories—or vice versa—and they kept each other laughing. It eased the inherent tensions of working in a war zone, helping everyone relax.

The last Sunday before the Elliotts traveled north with the McDonnalls and Karen Watson, another Southern Baptist worker, to scout potential water projects, they all gathered together for worship. Carrie strummed her guitar; David shared some Bible verses. "We sang the hymn, 'Nothing but the Blood,' and some choruses, prayed for guidance and wisdom in our work, and prayed that Jesus would be glorified in Iraq," Carrie says.

Jean had alerted her family back home of their journey to survey project sites in the north. "If you don't hear from us you will know that we are traveling and may not be able to get on-line," she wrote. "I have so much to tell you but will have to wait until there is more time. … We love you all very much! Thank you for remembering us …

"Our love, Mom and Dad"

It was her last e-mail.

On March 14, Larry submitted an exciting project proposal for a training center to aid handicapped Iraqis. But he never had a chance to follow up on it. The next day, the group drove through the Mosul area, in the vicinity of the ancient site of Nineveh. Iraqis there needed clean water and were grateful that the Americans cared for their plight. Larry surveyed needs and jotted notes on how he could assist. Jean enjoyed the local hospitality. "We had a great day with them," Carrie says.

As they continued traveling in the area later that day, a vehicle pulled alongside. Gunmen—probably insurgents or local thugs targeting foreigners—fired automatic weapons into their truck, hitting all five Southern Baptist workers multiple times. Larry and Jean died at the scene; so did Karen Watson. David McDonnall died hours later. Carrie McDonnall, grievously wounded, would eventually recover.

Why did God call Larry and Jean Elliott to Iraq?

Why did He call them home so soon after their arrival, when they had so much wisdom and experience and love to give to a needy nation?

One might as well ask why Jesus' public ministry lasted only three years. Larry and Jean were allowed to give three fruitful decades to missions and ministry.

"I don't like being the daughter of martyrs," Gina admits. "I miss them. We all miss them. But God has been faithful. Mom always used to say, 'God is good. He's good all the time.' He is the Father of the fatherless, and He takes care of you."

WHAT WOULD LARRY AND JEAN SAY?
IF GOD TELLS YOU TO DO SOMETHING,
DO IT—JOYFULLY.

God knows why. Perhaps one day in glory He will tell us. We do know that their lives of love blessed thousands—and their deaths have inspired and challenged many more.

What would Larry and Jean say? Carl Rees guesses it might be something like this: If God tells you to do something, do it—joyfully. They never shied away from hard work, or hard places. If it weren't hard, anybody could do it. It takes a servant to get down in the mud to drill a well—or hug a hurting people—and come up smiling.

That was Larry and Jean.

"People wanted to follow them—I wanted to follow them—because they followed Jesus with a wholehearted devotion," said pastor John Durham, an old friend, at a memorial service.

"There is fruit to a life that is wholly yielded to God."

KAREN WATSON

love letters to God

Karen 7 Watson

The letter—written a year and a week before Karen Watson died March 15, 2004—said it all.

It made international news in the days after anonymous gunmen killed Karen and three other Southern Baptist workers as they were surveying sites for humanitarian projects in northern Iraq.

"Missionary slain in Iraq mourned," read the headline in the *Los Angeles Times*. "In letter Karen Watson wrote to her church, she penned her own epitaph."

Phil Neighbors, one of her pastors at Valley Baptist Church in Bakersfield, Calif., found the short letter—in a sealed envelope marked "Open in case of death"—among some things Karen left with the church when she departed for the Middle East.

Standing in the Valley Baptist pulpit—above a large, framed photograph of Karen's smiling face and the casket that contained her body—Neighbors read the handwritten note to more than 1,000 people who attended her funeral service. It said in part:

Dear Pastor Phil and Pastor Roger,

You should only be opening this in the event of death.

When God calls there are no regrets. I tried to share my heart with you as much as possible, my heart for the nations. I wasn't called to a

*place; I was called to Him. To obey was my objective, to suffer was
expected, His glory my reward, His glory my reward …*

The missionary heart:

> *Cares more than some think is wise*
> *Risks more than some think is safe*
> *Dreams more than some think is practical*
> *Expects more than some think is possible*

I was called not to comfort or to success but to obedience. …

*There is no Joy outside of knowing Jesus and serving Him. I love
you two and my church family.*

In His care,

Salaam, Karen

"TO OBEY WAS MY OBJECTIVE, TO SUFFER WAS
EXPECTED, HIS GLORY MY REWARD. I WAS
CALLED NOT TO COMFORT OR TO SUCCESS
BUT TO OBEDIENCE. …"

Amid their tears, listeners could be forgiven for jumping to the
conclusion that Karen somehow knew before she ever left the United States that she would never come home alive. Phil Neighbors,
who knew her well, insists that wasn't the case.

"I don't believe she was being mystical, or that she had a premo-
nition that she would die," he says. "She was being practical. She was
taking care of business."

Karen knew how to take care of business. Hers—and yours if
you didn't step lively. Ask anybody who worked with her.

She also knew she was heading into a dangerous region where anything could happen. She sold her house and her car before leaving, gave away most of her other belongings. She was thrilled about this adventurous new chapter of her life and anticipated long-term service. But she was tying up loose ends—just in case. In her letter, she even told her pastors how to handle her funeral.

"In regards to any service, keep it small and simple," she directed.

"Just preach the gospel. If Jason Buss is available or his dad, have them sing a pretty song. Be bold and preach the life-saving, life-changing, forever eternal GOSPEL. Give glory and honor to our Father."

The instructions were classic Karen: Take charge, get it done, do it right. You can almost imagine her warning from heaven: "Don't make me come down there and do it for you!"

Pastor Phil and Pastor Roger (Spradlin) faithfully carried out her wishes at the funeral. They preached the gospel—loud and clear. Pastor Phil led seekers in the congregation in the sinner's prayer and gave an invitation; a number of mourners raised their hands and gave their hearts to Jesus. Karen's friend Jason Buss sang a pretty song, just as she wanted. Above all, the service glorified and honored the Lord.

But "keep it small and simple" was one request the church couldn't quite fulfill. Too many people loved Karen. Too many people —family members, hundreds of church members and friends, missionaries, six full rows of deputies from the Kern County Sheriff's Department—wanted to pay tribute to her and celebrate her life.

Small was out of the question. So was simple.

Karen wasn't a simple person. Her journey from multiple per-

sonal tragedies to vital faith in God—and ultimately martyrdom—
isn't a simple story.

"She wasn't perfect. She had issues just like us," says Barbara
Schmidt, a close friend and staff member at Valley Baptist. "She was
a real person. She was a hero, but she wouldn't want us to consider
her a hero without giving the glory to God."

Many times during her 38 years of life, Karen—like so many
children of broken homes—battled anger and bitterness, depression
and loneliness, perfectionism and insecurity, the compulsion to rebel
against authority. She also struggled with fear in Iraq—and freely
admitted it.

"DON'T MAKE KAREN INTO A SAINT.
SHE WOULD HATE THAT. SHE WAS PRETTY
WILD WHEN SHE WAS YOUNG. BUT WHEN SHE
BECAME A CHRISTIAN, SHE TURNED AROUND
180 DEGREES."

But courage isn't the absence of fear, as Pastor Roger reminded
listeners at the funeral. Courage is the laying aside of fear to obey
God, trusting Him with the consequences.

Was she a saint?

"Don't make Karen into a saint," urges another friend. "She
would hate that. She was pretty wild when she was young. But when
she became a Christian, she turned around 180 degrees."

That's actually a pretty good definition of biblical sainthood—if
a saint is a repentant sinner saved by grace, never fully at home in

this world, never too comfortable in one's own skin, always striving to serve God. Consider Simon Peter, or Mary Magdalene, or Martin Luther. Read the *Confessions* of St. Augustine—a hard-partying guy in a decadent age who wallowed in every form of sin before becoming one of the giants of Christian history.

So who, exactly, was Karen Watson? One tough gal, to hear some tell it. Before becoming a believer she managed a pool hall. She liked to drink in those days. If you made her mad, look out. Later, as an Emergency Response Unit member with the Kern County Sheriff's Department, she trained deputies to quell jail inmate disorder—by force if necessary.

Her tough skin, however, covered a heart that had suffered deep hurt and loss. She desperately wanted to love—and be loved.

Once Karen gave her heart to Jesus, He began the patient process of softening her—a process recorded in the journals she kept throughout her nine-year walk with God. Her journals are filled with insights from Bible studies, notes on sermons, quotes from devotional readings. But their essence is a series of love letters from God to Karen—and from Karen to God. He spoke to her through Scripture, His presence, people, life experiences. She spoke to Him in passionate, achingly honest written prayers.

They are her own psalms of praise, the record of her pursuit of God with all of her mind, body, and soul. That was her life's mission, after all, not church work or mission work. Remember the words in her letter: "I wasn't called to a place; I was called to Him. … His glory my reward. …"

LOVE AND LOSS

"Forgiveness is what I need most. Help me to forgive."
— *Karen's journal, December 3, 1995*

Karen Denise Watson was born June 18, 1965, at Mercy Hospital in Bakersfield, to parents Ted and Yvonne Watson.

"I remember the day we brought her home from the hospital," says her sister Lorraine, who was five years older. "She was just a ball of energy, happy-go-lucky, involved in everything. She never put off till tomorrow what she could do today. She was very determined."

That applied to everything—playing, school, sports, friendships. Total commitment. No turning back. Go for it. If it works, use it. If it's broken, fix it.

But there was one thing Karen couldn't fix: her own family. It was to be a lifelong source both of love and pain.

"She had a tough childhood … a lot of hurt," says Pastor Phil, who counseled and mentored Karen in later years.

Like so many children of the baby boom and Generation X, young Karen and her siblings found themselves caught in the break-up of a home and a marriage. In the aftermath, her father, whom she needed desperately, was gone. So was emotional security. Many lonely days followed.

"Mom raised us," adds Lorraine. "She worked a lot, sometimes three jobs, to support all of us. We never did without, but there were no extras. I looked after Karen. Wherever I went, she went. We did everything together."

Part protective big sister, part substitute mother, Lorraine did her best to look out for Karen, to smooth over the rough times. But as Karen grew, she became more and more determined to make her own way, build her own emotional shelters.

"I WOULD ALWAYS TRY TO FIX EVERYTHING FOR HER AS A KID. SHE WOULD ALWAYS SAY, 'WHY DO YOU TRY TO FIX EVERYTHING? LET ME MAKE MY OWN MISTAKES!'"

"I would always try to fix everything for her as a kid," Lorraine admits. "She would start to do something wrong and I would say, 'Don't do that!' She would always say, 'Why do you try to fix everything? Let me make my own mistakes!' So I had to back off as she got older and let her make her own decisions."

Karen was in control now, fully independent and on the loose. She finished high school, attended community college for a while, worked a series of jobs—often two or three at a time—to provide for herself. But the hole in her heart never fully closed.

And it would be torn far wider.

In the space of a few years as Karen raced into young adulthood, tragedy struck not once but three times. First her grandmother, whom she adored, was killed by a drunk driver in 1985. "We buried her two days before Christmas," Lorraine says.

Later, Karen re-established contact with her father, a reunion she had greatly longed for. But he, too, was killed in 1987 in a freak accident while cutting down a tree on his property.

Reeling from these losses, Karen met a man she thought would be the love of her life. She was managing a pool hall—and had promised herself she would never date any of the patrons. But a friend brought in a guy who challenged her to shoot a game. If she lost, she had to go out with him.

"Why not?" thought Karen, who knew her way around a pool table. "He can't beat me."

He won the game. So they went out.

"They fell deeply in love," recounts a close friend. "He had a horse, and they would go out riding together. He treated her like a queen. He was romantic; he sent her flowers and gave her gifts. He gave her affection and a sense of security, which she had never experienced before."

The happy couple began to talk about marriage. Karen also grew quite close to his parents. A happy home and family, Karen's long-cherished dream, seemed within her reach. Then, in a horrific attack, a deranged member of her boyfriend's family murdered him and his parents.

It was too much to bear. Karen could take no more heartbreak.

For months she could barely function. A Christian friend reached out to her as she struggled with almost catatonic despair. The friend took Karen in and cared for her during the darkest days.

FINDING HER TRUE FATHER

"I opened my heart (to a believer) about wanting to know Jesus and how scared I was. We talked on the phone for two and a half hours. … I asked God to be my Savior and come into my life. … The next morning my very first thought was of the Lord! I was so happy."
— Karen's journal, November 22, 1995

Slowly, slowly, Karen began to emerge from the depths. She returned to work and a semblance of normality. But her inner wounds were now too deep for her to go on without the Lord.

"That was a crisis point in her life," Pastor Phil says. "Things like that can make you better or bitter. For Karen, it made her better."

> "TOTAL EMPTINESS, ABSOLUTE LOSS AND HOPELESSNESS—THAT IS WHERE GOD BEGAN TO WORK. IT ALLOWED THIS HARD, HARD HEART TO BE OPEN TO HEARING WORDS OF LOVE FROM BELIEVERS."

It didn't happen overnight. It would take years. There were many layers of scar tissue to peel away. But the Divine Physician was at work. "It was not without a purpose that God was allowing this kind of suffering in her life," says a friend. "He was using it to bring her to Him. Total emptiness, absolute loss, and hopelessness—that is where God began to work. It allowed this hard, hard heart to be open to hearing words of love from believers."

Karen was known for asking tough, confrontational questions— of herself, of others, of life. Now she was asking them of God. "She had a lot of unanswered questions after these deaths," Lorraine recalls. "'What's going to happen to us when we die?' A lot of things started coming up. She needed more in her life, so she started going to church."

First she attended a small congregation called Grace Community Church. Later she moved to Valley Baptist, a fast-growing congregation in Bakersfield. Christians in both places met Karen where she was—in the midst of her search for answers. They loved her, patiently listened to her, answered the questions they could, and directed her toward the Lord for answers to the others.

One night in November of 1995 (see journal quote above), Karen found the answer she needed most. Stepping out in faith, she gave her fears and hurts to Christ and asked Him to become her Savior and Lord.

"How wonderful it was for me to find the love of Jesus to envelop me when I thought there was no hope left," she later wrote of that moment. "I remember feeling like the weight of the world was lifted off of my shoulders. He gave me a new heart that grew a love it had never known possible. I was hungry for God's Word and for fellowship with His people."

"FROM THE MOMENT SHE BECAME A CHRISTIAN, SHE BEGAN TO HUNGER FOR THE THINGS OF GOD AND LONG FOR A DEEP WALK WITH HIM."

A few months later, Karen was baptized. She gave her testimony of God's grace during the service, and asked that her new favorite song be sung. It wasn't a hymn about God's comforting love or the blessed assurance He gives Christians, as one might expect of a new believer recovering from years of pain. Rather, it was a missionary song, a call to obedience: "Here am I, Send me to the Nations." Even at the beginning of her walk with God, Karen sensed God's purpose for her—and for all of His children.

"From the moment she became a Christian, she began to hunger for the things of God and long for a deep walk with Him," says Pastor

Phil. But that longing was accompanied by a desire to share the joy she had found with others.

"She immediately had a heart for outreach," Phil explains. "She got involved in our singles ministry and just showed natural leadership. She became active in singles outreach and visitation and led a lot of people to the Lord. When a person crosses that threshold and becomes a witnessing Christian, they're on their way to maturity. You have to reach that threshold or you plateau. There was no plateau in Karen's spiritual experience. She had her ups and downs, but she very quickly became a witnessing Christian."

Karen always loved kids, too. As she grew spiritually, she began teaching in children's Sunday School and Vacation Bible School. One of her favorite experiences: leading a 10-year-old boy to Christ during a VBS session. "He understood completely that he was a sinner and that the only way to forgiveness was to ask Jesus to forgive him," she wrote. "He willingly surrendered himself to the Lord, inviting Jesus into his heart to be Lord of his life."

Two years later, he volunteered to go on a mission trip to Belize.

SENSE OF JUSTICE, CALL TO SERVICE

"I'm not going to give anything to my Lord that will cost me nothing."
— *Karen's journal, August 20, 1998*

Karen Watson seldom did things the easy way.

During her first year as a believer, she embarked on a new career that challenged her to live out her growing faith. She had been working for the commissary service that delivered food to inmates housed at Kern County's jail facilities. Her outgoing nature and out-spoken opinions won her numerous friends among the sheriff's deputies who ran the jail. She was offered a job as a detention officer with the Sheriff's Department—and she seized the opportunity.

Karen had a deep sense of justice, of right and wrong, which had been violated many times during her years of pain. Law enforcement represented a way to try to right some of those wrongs. And as a young Christian, Karen had by no means become a quiet, retiring nun. She was still Karen: in charge—and when she felt it necessary —in your face.

"SHE WAS A STRAIGHT SHOOTER. SHE DIDN'T SUGARCOAT ANYTHING; SHE TOLD YOU HOW IT WAS."

"She was a straight shooter. She didn't sugarcoat anything; she told you how it was," says Lt. Kevin Wright, her commanding officer and closest friend in the department. "She had one speed and that was 100 miles per hour. When you were with Karen you either got onboard the train or you were left behind. If she believed passion-ately about something, she'd let you know about it. I would hear her footsteps coming down the hall and know I was going to get a lec-ture about something. She would come in, close the door, sit on my desk and say, 'We gotta talk.'"

Despite their friendship, she once filed a grievance against him when he issued a departmental directive she opposed on principle.

"She said, 'Don't take it personally,' " Wright remembers with a chuckle. "I said, 'OK.' She felt like it was something she had to do."

Karen did her best at all times and expected everyone else to do the same. No slack, no excuses. Nearly everyone in the department liked her, though, because she backed her words with action, commitment, and loyalty. "She was the kind of person you wanted on your side when the going got rough," Wright says.

And things could get rough at times. Kern County is one of the largest in California. Its jail system is one of the 20 biggest in the nation and handles offenders of every type. Karen's duties over the years included new inmate intake and classification at a facility that housed 1,200 male prisoners. It was far more than a clerical duty; inmate interviews and intelligence gathering often identified criminal gang affiliations and other factors that could make the difference between calm and trouble in the jail. She became one of the first members of the department's Emergency Response Unit, which handles riot control and forced cell extractions. She learned—and trained other officers in—self-defense, use of firearms and stun guns, negotiating, and other methods for defusing trouble.

"She always wanted to better herself and train in whatever was available," Wright says. "She taught different classes in our academies and became one of my best training officers. Anytime we had a new trainee who seemed to be struggling, I would put them with Karen because I knew she would do her best for them."

Inmates liked her, too. She was firm, but fair.

"She was compassionate with them," Wright says. "They knew they weren't going to pull anything over on her, that she was strict and would enforce the rules. But she was willing to listen to them."

She took her work seriously. But she was also fun to be around. She baked goodies for deputies, kidded around, enjoyed finding

some good Mexican food after work shifts. Her strong sense of ca-
maraderie and teamwork marked her not only as a leader in the department, but also as a friend.

As time passed, though, her fellow officers realized a deeper
commitment was claiming Karen's heart and mind. She asked for
Sunday shifts off so she could worship at Valley Baptist. She became
involved in an Arab mission congregation begun by the church. In
addition to her ongoing outreach ministries, she began coordinating
church mission promotion materials—including a 70-foot-long
wall display dedicated to missions. The church was already committed to missions, but she challenged it to do more, at home and
abroad. "We ought to be welcoming sinners, not sin," she wrote at
the time. "Our church should be a birthing center" for redeemed
souls.

"She just fell in love with missionaries; she thought they were the
greatest people in the world," Pastor Phil recalls. "She became extremely active in missions education in our church and in promot-
ing Lottie Moon (Christmas Offering for International Missions).
She would come in here, sit down and say, 'We're not doing enough.
Let's get with the program!' So I turned a lot of that over to her because she could take the ball and run with it."

She also took time off from work to visit the Holy Land and go
on mission trips with Valley Baptist.

First came Mexico, then two trips to El Salvador and a journey
to Kosovo, Macedonia, and Greece. On her first trip to El Salvador,
in early 2001, the volunteer team led by Pastor Phil had barely
checked into their hotel when a major earthquake hit the tiny Central American country. It terrified Karen and the other team mem-

bers. They huddled in room doorways, then cowered in the street, as the quake rumbled and shook buildings violently. Instead of leaving when it was over, however, the team stayed to help provide relief aid and comfort to the people—even as aftershocks continued for days.

> "I LOVE YOU SO, FATHER, AND I WANT SO TO
> LOVE YOU ALL THE DAYS OF MY LIFE.
> HELP THESE HURT AND BROKEN PEOPLE. GIVE
> ME YOUR WORDS AND SPEAK THROUGH EACH
> OF US ... I FEEL SO STRONGLY ABOUT BEING
> HERE, EVEN WHEN I AM FEARFUL!"

"We prayed with so many that need water," Karen wrote in her journal during the trip. "One lady had a friend with little ones who were buried in the landslide. ... One little girl received Christ. ... I love You so, Father, and I want so to love You all the days of my life. Help these hurt and broken people. Give me Your words and speak through each of us. ... I feel so strongly about being here, even when I am fearful!"

When she returned home from her second trip to El Salvador a year later, she penned this entry: "I am once again left challenged. What will I do with the rest of my life? Serve the world? Or serve God? Go into ministry? Go to the mission field? What is God calling me to do? How can I serve my Master, Father, Savior better? God help me to recognize when it is You calling, and not just me wanting."

As the months passed—and her passion grew—she realized ever more clearly that it was God calling.

I SURRENDER ALL

"For the sake of the call. Reckless abandon. Abandon it all.

No other reason at all. ... Draw me close, sweet Savior. Jesus, lover of my soul, draw me to Thee. I need You now more than ever. I surrender all. ... I can look back and see Your hand drawing me to You and to these people. A purpose. Thank you for my purpose."

— Karen's journal, March 9, 2003, aboard a flight departing
Los Angeles for the Middle East

Wherever she went, whomever she met, Karen made a strong impression. Southern Baptist workers in the Middle East heard about Karen long before she arrived in their midst. Staff members at the International Mission Board told them about a dynamic gal from California.

"You really need to talk to this young lady," one staffer urged. "She's interested in your part of the world. You ought to grab her if you can."

They described a person who had multiple skills, a deep love for the Arab people she was ministering to through her church—and a profound call to service.

"I believe God has called me to full-time international missions, giving me a heart full of love for lost and hurting people of other cultures," Karen had written in her application for missionary service. "I believe God has had His hand on my life from the time of my conversion, placing me in just the right places with the right people who also have a heart for the lost."

A team leader from the region met with Karen at the International Mission Board's offices in Richmond, Virginia, where she was attending a conference for candidates exploring various service opportunities. The war in Iraq had not yet begun, but the reality of it seemed certain. Christian workers in the region anticipated that when it was over, the Iraqi people would need a lot of help to recover and rebuild. They wrote a job description for a humanitarian aid coordinator to be based in the area. It called for someone who could work under pressure with other team members, develop contacts and effective relationships with Iraqi officials and other humanitarian agencies (religious and secular), coordinate food aid and relief supply shipments, initiate rebuilding projects and assist in placement of other workers and volunteers.

That was for starters.

Despite her relative lack of overseas experience, Karen seemed an ideal fit for the two-year International Service Corps assignment. Her law enforcement career and numerous church ministries demonstrated her ability to lead a variety of people, train others, operate under potentially dangerous conditions, handle security arrangements, and juggle multiple duties.

"THAT GIRL COULD COORDINATE ANYTHING."

"That girl could coordinate anything," testifies Pastor Phil.

When the team leader outlined the job for Karen, she responded without hesitation: "Let's do it!"

She sold her house and car, sold or gave away most of her other possessions—whatever wouldn't fit in a large duffel bag. After her official commissioning by the International Mission Board, and six weeks of International Service Corps training, she headed out.

"She was so excited," says Lorraine Gonzales, a friend from Valley Baptist who drove her to the airport. "She knew she was doing the right thing."

First, however, it was hurry up and wait. She had to acclimate herself to the Middle East, study basic Arabic language and culture—and wait out the invasion phase of the battle for Iraq—from a neighboring country. She met as many Iraqis as she could find there, visiting in homes, drinking tea, listening to their stories of hardship. She stayed with another Southern Baptist family assigned to the area and watched the war next-door on TV, preparing for whatever doors of ministry that might soon open in Iraq.

"We fell in love with her, because she was so real," says a member of the family. "She talked about her struggles and the things she was excited about. She had character—and a little bit of an attitude—but such a commitment to the Lord Jesus Christ. We enjoyed watching her grow in her love for Arabs."

A month later, she set up shop in Kuwait City, where numerous non-governmental organizations (NGOs) and aid groups were rushing to open offices and staging areas in anticipation of starting relief work in postwar Iraq.

Amid the chaos, Karen was an island of order—as much order, at least, as she could bring to a situation that changed daily and often hourly. "Show me Your path, that I may follow it straight," she wrote in her journal. "Show us what is most important to You. Not stuff, plans and details, but You, O Lord."

She obtained NGO status and office space for the Southern Baptist relief team. The team itself was far from organized at that point, with multiple workers based in multiple countries. She attended countless meetings with government officials, United Nations officials, aid agencies, military liaison officers. She kept other team members informed of what was developing and what kinds of assistance would be most strategic when they got into Iraq.

"She worked long, long hours," says a colleague. "It was logistical things. It was establishing relationships with other NGOs and U.N. people and getting on top of security issues for our people. She knew practically everybody in Kuwait who had any ties to Iraq. It's amazing to me given her lack of experience, because NGO-type stuff can be a maze even for long-time professionals—and she was out there on her own in a lot of ways. She wasn't easily intimidated."

Above all, she made friends.

"In any type of work, it's really the relationships you build, and she was a very relational person," one of her supervisors explains. "Especially in Kuwait as we were setting up there, women from the U.S. military's Humanitarian Operations Center (HOC) and others would come to our office and just sit for hours. Karen put a little refrigerator in there with drinks and stuff, and they'd come in there to get away. It was sort of a safe place where they could hang out with Karen."

Once, the HOC chief paid a personal visit and said, "You know what? Every other agency that comes here has some kind of complaint. But I've never heard anything from you guys but praise. You seem content with what you are doing and happy about something." It gave Karen and her colleagues an opportunity to share why the Lord had sent them there.

BAGHDAD

"Trust and faith—I mustn't forget that. I was so tired from being up so late and I wanted to sleep. ... Father, I am so grateful for all Your protection over me. Thank you for sustaining me the way You do. For- give me when I sin and fail."
— Karen's journal, August 7, 2003

Within weeks of the fall of Saddam Hussein's regime, Karen was in Baghdad with the first wave of relief workers.

According to one colleague, she essentially "ran the show" dur- ing the early days—obtaining lodging and work space for incom- ing Southern Baptist workers and volunteers, making contacts with Iraqis, hiring drivers and guards, monitoring security. She attended frequent meetings with United Nations and Coalition Provisional Authority representatives to discuss security and the most critical needs of Iraqis.

When relief work began in earnest, she worked with others to coordinate the distribution of thousands of food boxes sent by Southern Baptist churches and the rebuilding of damaged schools, among numerous other projects. One of her most cherished min- istries: the "Widows Project," a three-phase program that helped mostly illiterate Iraqi women learn to read, gain work skills, and generate income. It continues today and has spread throughout Iraq.

Once again, her most important contribution was making friends.

"Karen built relationships everywhere she went, whether she was negotiating a contract for a house or talking to someone about being employed as a guard," says a colleague. "People remember her. They remember the light in her countenance. They remember her friendliness."

Through her contacts at high levels, Karen made friends with some of the most influential women in Iraq—women who were experiencing the breath of freedom for the first time in their lives.

"I do see an open door here that is unique," she wrote to a friend in August. "I was just at a meeting for women yesterday. ... They have choices for the first time and they just don't know what to do. They asked me to speak and I was able to tell them what our NGO does and some of its projects. I told them how proud we were that they were forming to make a difference in the lives of the community here ... Some of these women are highly educated—multiple PhDs. I told them I was not here to teach them anything (but) to learn and listen and help support them as women."

"I HAVE MET SPECIAL LADIES IN MY NEIGHBORHOOD WHO JUST WANT SOMEONE TO TALK TO AND HAVE TEA WITH. THEY WANT TO TELL THEIR STORY OF PAIN. THEY JUST FEEL SO FREE. I WANT FOR THEM THE REAL FREEDOM OF OUR LORD."

She also had made friends among Iraqi women where she lived: "I have met many special ladies in my neighborhood who just want someone to talk to and have tea with. They want to tell their story of pain. They just feel so free. I want for them the real freedom of our Lord. I think there are seekers here and people of peace. At the same time, there is a spiritual battle that is thick. I know I have never experienced it before."

The spiritual battle only intensified for Karen and her co-workers as the brutally hot summer months of 2003 passed. Threats against foreigners were increasing. The terrorist and insurgent network was becoming better organized—and determined to drive out not only coalition military forces but also foreign relief and reconstruction workers.

Karen personally experienced several close calls in the Baghdad area as bombings and street attacks mounted. On the morning of

> "U.N. BOMBING, BAGHDAD. THE HORROR OF IT ALL—HOW MANY WILL DIE? ... I THINK OF THEIR ETERNITY ... WE ALL KNOW PEOPLE THERE. WE JUST KEEP GOING ON. ISN'T THAT WHAT YOU DO IN A CRISIS?"

August 19, she attended a meeting at U.N. headquarters in Baghdad. She had felt uncomfortable about the relative lack of security at the building for some time. That day she felt especially uneasy and left as soon as she could. That afternoon, a truck bomb ripped the building apart, killing more than 20 people (including Sergio de Mello, the U.N. special envoy to Iraq) and injuring hundreds. It marked the bloody beginning of a terror campaign against foreign civilians that would continue indefinitely.

"U.N. bombing, Baghdad," Karen wrote in her journal that night. "Once again I am reminded of His hand of protection. … The horror of it all—how many will die? … I think of their eternity. … We all know people there. We just keep going on. Isn't that what you do in a crisis? Push forward, move ahead. Lord, I am so glad I am in this place. I am so glad Your timing is perfect because You alone are perfect."

Karen was glad to be there, but the heightening tension began to take a toll. The work went on, but the ongoing chaos frustrated her desire to run an efficient operation. The gunfire woke her up at night; sleep seldom returned. The growing violence and terror weighed on her more than some of her co-workers—and not just because she was a single woman, though that made it even harder for her to function in Iraq. Professionally trained to be alert to security issues, she took her responsibility for the safety of the whole team very seriously. She read daily updates from the authorities, talked to her many contacts about the latest threats, continually weighed the ongoing risks and opportunities. It became overwhelming.

"She was burning out," observes a team member and friend. "Karen was at her best in difficult circumstances, but it was emotionally exhausting for her. When we heard from her, she was either really angry or in tears and feeling despair. On top of that, I can't begin to describe the type of spiritual warfare that surrounds this particular people group. The enemy was definitely trying to discourage her."

By September of 2003, Karen knew she had to get out—at least for a while.

"I have had many difficult decisions to make recently concerning the work here," she wrote to a supervisor September 9. "Despite the growing guerrilla warfare, the people are wonderful. … I have had to wrestle with what God wants me to do. It has been hard. It is with much heartache that I write this: I am going to (a neighboring country). I do pray that things will once again be settled here and that it will be safe to live and work here. … Thank you for your love and support. I really need it now."

When she reached the relative calm of the nearby country's capital, she confided to a co-worker there that she might never return to Iraq.

CHRIST'S BRIDE

"Lord, I want to work my heart into such a state that it has no will of its own. God, what way is my path to go? Show me and I will follow You, Lord. Make it abundantly clear. In Ecclesiastes You say there is a time for all things and certainly a purpose. Show me day by day what You want me to do."

— Karen's journal, February 25, 2004

For a time, Karen rested—mentally, physically, spiritually.

She savored the feeling of having lunch with friends at McDonald's without having to look over her shoulder or listen for explosions and gunfire. She studied Arabic. She spent many hours in Scripture and prayer.

In late October, "Salaam," an Iraqi Muslim co-worker, was shot and critically wounded by Saddam loyalists—retaliation for working in relief projects Karen had helped initiate in northern Iraq. Karen knew his chances for survival were slim in Iraq. She used all of her contacts and coordinating skills to pull off a near-miraculous emergency air evacuation. Salaam was transported to a modern medical facility in the city where she was living.

Ironically, Karen and Salaam had locked horns more than once in Iraq. He thought she was too pushy and controlling. She was irritated by his more relaxed approach. But as he struggled for life in his hospital bed, Karen became his guardian and protector.

"Karen visited Salaam every day, sometimes two and three times a day," a friend recounts. "On several occasions after he was transferred out of the ICU, she arrived just as he was struggling to breathe because his tracheotomy tube was clogged. She would call for help and an inexperienced nurse would come and say there's nothing wrong. Karen would cry, 'Look at him, he's dying! You have to help him!' She would run back up to the ICU and get an experienced nurse to come."

"Karen made trouble at the hospital because of me," Salaam testifies. "Many times she saved my life."

She arranged for Salaam's wife and four children to come to the country from a village in Iraq and found a place for them to live. "Karen took care of my family," he says. "I couldn't afford to put them in school, but she found a school for them."

Remembering their testy relationship in Iraq, Salaam finally asked Karen, "Why do you do this? Why are you coming to see me?"

"Because God put a love for the Iraqi people in my heart, and He has given me a love for you," she told him.

"Karen looked at me with the face of an angel," Salaam says.

When he recovered enough to talk more, he had the joy of telling her good news. "When I was in Iraq I did not believe in Jesus, but a miracle happened to me. I was not a praying man, but the day before I was shot, I prayed all day. On the way to the hospital, I saw Jesus with me in the ambulance. Now I am with Jesus. Karen was the first person I told when I came (here)."

As months passed, Karen confronted her anxieties about Iraq and what was happening there. She prayed and studied key passages of God's Word with two close friends and co-workers—grappling once again not only with current fears but with old wounds and heartbreak.

"Rejoice to the extent that you partake of Christ's sufferings, that when His glory is revealed, you may also be glad with exceeding joy," she wrote in her journal, quoting the Apostle Paul's triumphant anthem of faith in 2 Corinthians 4. "Our light affliction, which is but for a moment, is working for us a far more exceeding and eternal weight of glory. The fellowship of His sufferings. We are created to be in the likeness of His Son Jesus.

"SHE WAS WALKING IN TOTAL BROKENNESS AND SURRENDER. SHE HAD A WOUNDED HEART, BUT A HEART FULL OF CHRIST. GOD HAD STRIPPED HER OF EVERYTHING, ALL SUPPORT SYSTEMS. IT WAS JUST KAREN AND GOD."

"Lord, in all my weakness I need Your strength for the future. ..."
Hard pressed, but not crushed. Perplexed, but not in despair.

Persecuted, but not abandoned. Struck down, but not destroyed. This was the normal Christian life, as Paul taught and lived it, the life through which God demonstrates His power and glory in our fragile jars of clay.

"She was walking in total brokenness and surrender," remembers a close friend. "She had a wounded heart, but a heart full of Christ. God had stripped her of everything, all support systems. It was just Karen and God. There's nothing more beautiful to watch than someone who is completely broken; nothing mattered to her anymore except God and Him being glorified. It brought incredible healing to her heart."

Karen made two brief trips back to Iraq for team meetings, enduring the gut-wrenching corkscrew descents pilots follow to avoid being shot down by insurgents as they land in Baghdad. Conditions there were just as challenging, if not more so. She still had security concerns. But Karen was convinced it was time to return. "I'm going back," she told her friend and prayer partner before heading to Baghdad for the last time.

Shortly before she left, Karen bought a beautiful gold ring with several small diamonds. The purchase surprised friends, since Karen usually saved much of her small salary and lived on next to nothing.

"It looked like a wedding band," says her friend. "She came to my house for dinner the night before I took her to the airport, and she was wearing it on the ring finger of her left hand. I wore a wedding band before I got married, too, to remind me that Christ was my husband, that I wasn't alone."

She asked Karen if that was what she had in mind.

"Yes," Karen replied with a radiant smile. "I guess that's it."

When Karen got back to Baghdad, she barely had time to unpack before heading north to scout potential aid projects with co-workers David and Carrie McDonnall and new arrivals Larry and Jean Elliott. She was wary about traveling into the dangerous areas around Mosul, an old Saddam stronghold, but seemed "happy and at peace" about being back, according to one of the workers who welcomed her. She was especially excited about working with Larry Elliott—an expert in water purification with long experience in aiding poor communities and disaster victims in Central America. With him onboard, better days were coming for the Iraqi people she loved so much. Clean water to drink. Living Water for new life.

The night of March 13, Karen called her close friend from a city in northern Iraq.

"She was so joyful; she just went on and on," her friend recounts. "She said, 'I can't believe how glad I am that I made this trip.' She was as happy as I had ever heard her." The next day they were heading for Mosul, where many people needed the help they could bring. She couldn't wait to go.

Two days later, the small truck carrying Karen, the McDonnalls and the Elliotts was riddled with bullets on a road outside Mosul. Karen died at the scene, as did the Elliotts. David McDonnall died hours later. Critically wounded, Carrie survived and recovered.

WEDDING DAY

When Karen's friend learned of her death, she wept along with everyone else. Then she thought of the wedding ring—and her weeping turned to tears of celebration:

"I thought of Stephen's martyrdom (in the book of Acts), and I realized that was the only place in Scripture where Christ, seated at the right hand of God, stands to receive someone into heaven. That

> "I DON'T KNOW IF I HAVE EVER BEEN WITH ANYONE WHO WAS MORE READY TO MEET HIM FACE TO FACE."

imagery came to me as I was praising Him for taking Karen home. It was her wedding day. He had so prepared her as a bride that she was completely without blemish. I don't know if I have ever been with anyone who was more ready to meet Him face to face."

Only Karen—and her beloved Bridegroom—know all the reasons why she returned to Iraq, and why she died there. He is still there, however. His Spirit is moving across the land to accomplish His purposes amid the suffering and turmoil. Through the storm, many Iraqis are feeling the wind of freedom upon their cheeks. Freedom from terror and oppression. Freedom to make their own choices, like the women of Baghdad Karen encouraged. Freedom to seek the truth that truly makes one free—regardless of what happens in the political realm.

As they seek, they won't forget Karen Watson, who laid aside her fear and sacrificed everything that they might be free. But in the end, her joyful sacrifice wasn't for them.

It was for Him.

IRAQ AFTERWORD

"Thus says the Lord, 'Yet again there will be heard in this place, of which you say, "It is a waste, without man and without beast" … the voice of joy and the voice of gladness, the voice of the bridegroom and the voice of the bride, the voice of those who say, "Give thanks to the Lord of hosts, for the Lord is good, for His lovingkindness is everlasting". … For I will restore the fortunes of the land as they were at first,' says the Lord." (Jeremiah 33:10, 11)

Jeremiah prophesied about the Lord's merciful, restoring love toward desolate Jerusalem. Yet does He not continue to extend mercy toward the land of Nineveh, the disobedient city He loved, the city that repented in sackcloth and ashes when His reluctant servant Jonah went there with His offer of reconciliation?

The ruins of Nineveh lie near present-day Mosul. Near the place where Karen Watson died joyfully following her Bridegroom. Where David McDonnall and Larry Elliott were last heard to laugh. Where Jean Elliott last smiled and hugged a child.

They brought the love of God to a land He still loves just as much as He loved Nineveh. Violence continues there more than a year after they died, but the still, small voice of His Spirit is being heard by Iraqis. The love expressed by Karen, David, Larry, Jean, and many others is reaching more and more people.

"God created me—and you—to live with a single, all-embracing, all-transforming passion," writes John Piper in his book, Don't Waste Your Life. *"Namely, a passion to glorify God by enjoying and displaying His supreme excellence in all the spheres of life … The wasted life is*

the life without a passion for the supremacy of God in all things for the joy of all peoples."

David, Karen, Larry, and Jean lived life with that kind of passion. Carrie continues to live life that way—and challenges others to do the same. This is the kind of life God intends for us, however long or short it may be. Anything less is a waste.

Is it safe? No, not necessarily. God never promised it would be—in Iraq or anyplace else. Karen Watson anticipated suffering before she ever left home. So should we all.

"I'm not going to say this is a safe place," says a worker in Iraq. "If I did, I'd be lying. But it is a place that God wants to touch—and is touching—by His Spirit. We are to walk with God into these places where He is fighting the battle, because the victory is His."

Amen.

EPILOGUE: MAY WE WHO FOLLOW BE FOUND FAITHFUL

The pain is deep, the grief prolonged. We do not readily get over the abrupt loss of a colleague and friend. The death of a son or daughter, husband, father or brother, a wife, mother, or sister, leaves an ache in the depth of one's soul. The vibrant smile is gone; the hearty laugh is silent. The intimate sharing with a mentor and encourager has ceased. We cannot understand why one so devoted to serving the Lord would have his or her ministry cut short, or why the light of a testimony in a dark world would be extinguished.

Yes, we grieve. A missionary team feels a glaring gap when one of its numbers is no longer there. A family, who had become accustomed to separation and only occasional fellowship during a periodic furlough, struggles with the reality that a loved one will not be coming home on stateside assignment again. Our Lord identified with our grief in the loss of a friend, and we know that He identifies with us still. It is not incidental that His abiding presence in the person of the Holy Spirit would be identified as "the Comforter," the One who comes alongside us and brings peace to our troubled hearts and grace to minister to our need.

The Apostle Paul put this experience in perspective in 1 Thessalonians 4:13: "But we do not want you to be uninformed brethren, about those who are asleep, so that you will not grieve, as do the rest who have no hope." He is not saying that we should not grieve, but because we know our Lord and are assured of the eternal destiny of those who die in Him, our grief is not as those who have no hope.

Many of us have lived among those with no hope. Multitudes of Buddhists, striving for their eternal destiny through their own good works, may live a noble life. But at their funeral, the monks will encircle their casket chanting, "Dead never to arise; asleep never to awaken; gone never to return." I have witnessed Hindus gathering at the funeral pyre, weeping and wailing as their plethora of deities can offer no hope of deliverance from an endless cycle of reincarnations. Muslims, devout in their ritualistic prayers, serve a punitive god in a fatalistic abandonment to divine will. Humanists and secularists have no hope beyond this life, while animists are never free from their superstition and fears.

Why do missionaries risk their lives to go to dangerous places? It is to bring hope to those with no hope. It is to proclaim a God of love that offers eternal life to those in sin and despair.

We do not grieve as those without hope because we know our missionary friends gave their hearts to Jesus Christ as Savior years ago. We are comforted by the assurance that as they entered the presence of our Lord Jesus Christ, they were received with a cloak of righteousness, having been washed clean by the blood of the Lamb. How deep our grief would be if they had not made that decision, and we were left wondering about their relationship with God.

We do not grieve because they responded in obedience to God's call to give of their lives to reach a lost world and live for others. No, the glories of heaven become more of a reality when we think of their being welcomed by our Lord with the words, "Well done, good and faithful servant" (Matthew 25:21, NIV). We would be grieving more if they had neglected God's call and chosen to pursue the wealth and acclaim of the world, living for self and pleasure. But instead they gave of themselves that others might live. Only eternity will reveal the lives that were touched, the souls that were redeemed, and the influence their witness continues to bear.

> EACH OF THEM REPRESENTED A UNIQUE PILGRIMAGE OF FOLLOWING GOD WHEREVER HE LED AND A COMMITMENT TO OBEDIENCE WHATEVER THE COST. EACH OF US HAS A STEWARDSHIP TO RESPOND TO GOD'S CALL TO EMULATE THE LIFE AND DEVOTION THEY MODELED.

Neither can we grieve because of the influence that they had on those who knew them and countless others. We were blessed and inspired by their testimony. We were stirred by their devotion, their love for their Lord, and their passion for a lost world. We were enriched by their friendship and moved beyond our provincialism by the people in distant lands they came to love as their own. We often speak of the unique calling and devotion of those who go as missionaries; we speak of their sacrifice, their obedience, and their heart for the lost. To some degree it's true, but occasionally God allows us to go beyond the rhetoric and generic attributes we ascribe to missionaries to actually see one who walked with the Lord. Usually subsequent generations immortalize those who were used to impact our world, but we have been given the privilege of knowing personally some who one day will stand with Lottie Moon, Bill Wallace, and other heroes of the faith. Each of them represented a unique pilgrimage of following God wherever He led and a commitment to obedience whatever the cost. It is an example that continues to live and bear fruit, and each of us has a stewardship to respond to God's call to emulate the life and devotion they modeled.

In that impressive roll call of faith in the 11th chapter of Hebrews, it is said of Abel, but is true of all, *"though he is dead, he still speaks."* And the lives of those who died on the mission field continue to speak. The testimony of our three martyrs in Yemen continues to speak to those who observed their kind demeanor, heard them speak of a God they knew personally, and were recipients of their compassionate medical care. The testimonies of our four martyrs in Iraq continue to speak to the displaced and destitute Iraqis who welcomed them and opened the door for their water purification projects. The life and passion of Bill Hyde continue to speak through hundreds of church planters he trained and the multitudes who are coming to faith in Christ through those he discipled.

And they continue to speak to us, calling us to a new dimension of faithfulness and obedience. The memory of their desire to reach a lost world speaks to our hearts and encourages us to bring the priorities of our lives in line with God's desire to be exalted among the nations. Their abandonment to God's calling still speaks, challenging us to move beyond our conditional commitment and shallow devotion.

Many beautiful testimonies have been shared by their co-workers, friends, and families. It has been said on more than one occasion that these were people "of whom the world was not worthy." That expression comes from Hebrews 11:38, toward the conclusion of that familiar roll call of faith. It tells us that by faith Abel offered a more acceptable sacrifice, Enoch walked with God, Noah built the ark, Abraham followed God, Moses left the luxuries of Egypt to lead the people of God, and by faith the children of Israel passed through the Red Sea. We are told of Isaac and Jacob and Joseph, of Gideon and Samson and David and others who "by faith conquered kingdoms, performed acts of righteousness, obtained promises, shut the mouths of lions, quenched the power of fire, escaped the edge of the sword … put foreign armies to flight" (Hebrews 11:33-34).

What was it that made the world unworthy of these men and women?

First, their lives were not focused on this life, but on something of eternal significance. "[They were] looking for a city … whose architect and builder is God … a better country … a heavenly one. Therefore God is not ashamed to be called their God; for He has prepared a city for them" (Hebrews 11:10, 16).

Our missionaries, who were victims of terrorist gunfire and bombing, were not focused on the values and things of this life. Their passion was not aimed at attaining success and recognition. They had been trained and were very conscientious about issues of security, but their own safety was not the compelling priority of their lives. They understood the despair of people who were suffering; they comprehended the excessive darkness of hearts without Christ. They recognized the eternal consequences for those who had no opportunity to hear of God's love, and by faith they followed God and were obedient even unto death. They, like Moses, Abraham, and others, recognized they were strangers and exiles on earth, and they stayed focused on that promise of reward. For them, that reward was the day when there would be people—including Iraqis, Yemenis, and Filipinos—from every tribe and people and tongue and nation gathered around the throne and worshiping the Lamb of God.

When Carrie McDonnall, the one survivor of the Iraq tragedy, regained consciousness a week after the incident and was told that her husband, David, and the others had died, she said, "We have got to quit treating this life as home." She didn't expound on that statement, but apparently realized that as long as we look on this life as home we will be caught up in its values. We'll be seeking material comforts, worrying about our future, wondering how our investments

AS WE LOOK ON THIS LIFE AS HOME WE WILL BE CAUGHT UP IN ITS VALUES, SEEKING MATERIAL COMFORTS, WORRYING ABOUT OUR FUTURE, HOW OUR INVESTMENTS ARE DOING, BUILDING OUR HOMES, PREAPARING FOR A COMFORTABLE RETIREMENT, SEEKING FULFILLMENT IN THINGS OF THE WORLD.

are doing, building our homes, preparing for a comfortable retirement, seeking fulfillment in things of the world. Carrie, her husband, David, and their co-workers realized that there is something more important, more lasting, and more valuable. There is something worth giving your life for, and yes, worth dying for. Should not their example challenge us to become others of whom the world is not worthy?

Second, like Abraham, they followed God by faith. Abraham did not know where God was leading, but he followed by faith. That is not the way of the world. The world says, "Plan your life and follow your plan. Determine what you want to do. Pursue that which will bring you personal success and fulfillment." But "by faith, Abraham, when he was called, obeyed … and he went out, not knowing where he was going" (Hebrews 11:8).

Our parents have a problem when they see us making this kind of decision. They love us. They sincerely want what is best for us. They have invested in our education to enable us to be a successful doctor, teacher, or businessperson. Perhaps they have even celebrated our call to the ministry and taken pride in our serving the Lord in a church here in America. But to leave it all to go overseas doesn't make a lot of sense. Who would be so foolish as to obey God's call to engage an Unreached People Group, not knowing where you will live or whether there will be a hostile reception? But that doesn't really matter when your only concern is obedience and a willingness to trust God and follow Him by faith.

The world is not worthy of that kind of attitude. People don't understand it. It just doesn't fit the postmodern, self-centered philosophy and lifestyle that says it's all about me. It's not a matter of having to know where you are going. If you are to be one of whom the world is not worthy, you will not put a geographic restriction on where you are willing to serve the Lord, but will follow by faith wherever God leads and will keep your eyes on Him.

A third factor in being a person of whom this world is not worthy is to reject temporal pleasures and riches to identify with the people to whom God is leading you. Hebrews 11:24-26 tells us, "By faith Moses … choosing rather to endure ill-treatment with the people of God than to enjoy the passing pleasures of sin, considering the reproach of Christ greater riches than the treasures of Egypt …" It may mean selling the beautiful home of your dreams or walking away from a lucrative business or promising career. That's not the kind of decision that gets applauded by the world. It means accepting an austere lifestyle and giving up many of the amenities and comforts we take for granted here in America.

Larry and Jean Elliott's three children all testified to the wonderful legacy their parents had left them, a model of devotion and obedience to Christ. Larry left a prominent engineering career to go to Honduras, where they served for 25 years. His skills led him into relief work—drilling wells to provide pure drinking water, rebuilding homes and schools in the aftermath of Hurricane Mitch, providing sanitation to destitute and neglected villages. He gave his life for the sake of the people of Middle America, but primarily that they might have an eternal hope in Jesus Christ. I can assure you there is one thing the Elliott children have not had to do in the aftermath of the death of their parents. They have not had to deliberate on what they will do with a massive financial inheritance. Larry and Jean chose the risks, and they chose to live among the impoverished people of Honduras and the suffering of Iraq. They chose a meager missionary salary instead of the riches and treasures of an American lifestyle, for they, like Moses, knew there was a greater reward.

Finally, it means they did not shun suffering and death for the cause of Christ. We are told of heroes who won the prize, conquered kingdoms, escaped the sword, and obtained the promises. But there were others who "were tortured, not accepting their release, so that they might obtain a better resurrection; and others experienced mockings and scourgings, yes, also chains and imprisonment. They were stoned, they were sawn in two … they were put to death with the sword …" (Hebrews 11:35-37).

Reading this passage brings deep emotion and reverence. The Scripture tells us they could have avoided these consequences of their faith, but they chose not to accept their release—that they might obtain a better resurrection. They did not seek to avoid suffering and death for their own benefit. Nor did they put themselves in harm's way that they might have a martyr's crown, but that their witness would bear fruit and there would be a greater resurrection of those who believed.

WE NEED TO EXPLODE A PROMINENT AND OFT-QUOTED MYTH THAT THE SAFEST PLACE ON EARTH IS IN THE CENTER OF GOD'S WILL.

We need to explode a prominent and oft-quoted myth that the safest place on earth is in the center of God's will. Would we conclude that these victims of whom we have read were not in the center of God's will? Why do some die while others do not? Does God, in His providence, sort out, like the tares and the wheat, those who are in His will, placing a hedge of protection around them, while others are left vulnerable to the forces of an evil and fallen world? Not at all! In fact, Jesus said, "In this world you shall have tribulation" (John 16:33). He told His disciples, "… An hour is coming for everyone who kills you to think that he is offering service to God. These things they will do because they have not known the Father or Me!" (John 16:2-3). God does not put a hedge of protection and safety around us because we have answered His call. In fact, He does not guarantee that we will see response and success in our witness just because of our commitment. Our call is to obedience—period! Not for the sake of results, not for the assurance of safety, but for His glory and for His purpose to be fulfilled.

John and Betty Stam were missionaries serving with the China Inland Mission (now Overseas Missionary Fellowship) in 1934 when they were captured by communist forces expanding control throughout the country. John and Betty, seen as imperialistic foreigners collaborating with the Nationalist government, were held briefly and then beheaded. Other missionaries had met a similar fate, and the threat was real, although the Stams had mistakenly thought they were in a territory well removed from the danger. Being a prolific writer and poet, Betty reflected upon the prospects of losing their lives for the sake of a greater purpose and reward with these lines:

> *Afraid? Of What?*
> *To feel the spirit's glad release?*
> *To pass from pain to perfect peace,*
> *The strife and strain of life to cease?*
> *Afraid—of that?*

> *Afraid? Of What?*
> *Afraid to see the Savior's face,*
> *To hear His welcome, and to trace*
> *The glory gleam from wounds of grace?*
> *Afraid—of that?*

Afraid? Of What?
A flash, a crash, a pierced heart;
Darkness, light, O Heaven's art!
A wound of His a counterpart!
Afraid—of that?

Afraid? Of What?
To do by death what life could not—
Baptize with blood a stony plot,
Till souls shall blossom from the spot?
Afraid—of that?

[*To Die is Gain*, Westminster Literature Resources, Denton, Texas; pp. 104-105]

At Karen Watson's funeral, a friend reflected that she could tell something was happening in her life after each mission trip she went on. Finally, she resigned her job, sold her house, sold her car, and all her earthly possessions. She packed what was left in a duffel bag and headed for Iraq. A year later, her friend said, all that was left was her duffel bag, her Bible, and her devotion to Christ. Was it worth it? As Karen had written in that letter left with her pastor, "There are no regrets. My calling is to obedience, suffering is expected, His glory is my reward. ..." She expressed the attitude of our Savior who, contrary to others, knew the time of His martyrdom was approaching. He faced it, saying, "Father, the hour has come; glorify Thy Son, that the Son may glorify Thee." Karen was one of whom the world was not worthy. She did not shun suffering and death, but lived and died for God's glory.

We may not face a violent death that cuts short a long and fruitful life, but we, too, are challenged to be those of whom the world is not worthy—by focusing on values beyond this life. We also are to follow in obedience wherever God would lead, even though we do not know where and what the consequences will be. We should

> "THERE ARE NO REGRETS. MY CALLING IS TO OBEDIENCE, SUFFERING IS EXPECTED, HIS GLORY IS MY REWARD. ..."

consciously choose to reject the comforts, riches, and material values of this world in order to identify with the suffering, the lost, and the people for whom Christ died. And we must not reject the suffering that may accompany our calling. To do so may be to forfeit the greater reward and deprive God of the glory that accrues when we give Him our all.

Yes, the center of God's will is the safest place to be after all—not necessarily safe from the threats and dangers of this life, but the safest place to assure an eternal reward.

Our world continues to experience repercussions from the tragedy of September 11, 2001. It shattered our sense of security. We have been thrown into a neurosis of fear and suspicion. Tension and uncertainty have crumpled confidence in the future. Our economy is in disarray, global alliances are strained, and we struggle to understand religious worldviews that incite hatred and generate terrorist strategies of destruction and harm. But this kind of world is not without precedent. In fact, it is the same kind of hostile environment that the early believers faced in the book of Acts. Rulers and religious fanatics conspired to eradicate the fledgling Christian movement with the same determination as totalitarian governments and modern-day terrorists. Christians were persecuted, harassed, threatened, put in prison, and martyred.

Their prayer in the context of this situation is similar to the questions we are asking today in the aftermath of the loss of our missionary colleagues. In Acts 4:24-26 we read, "… They lifted their voices to God … and said, 'O Lord, it is You who made the heaven and the earth … and all that is in them, who by the Holy Spirit through the mouth of our father David Your servant, said, Why did the Gentiles rage, and the peoples devise futile things? The kings of the earth took their stand, and the rulers were gathered together against the Lord and against His Christ.'"

Should we expect our world to be any different today? Why do the nations rage and devise futile things? Why do the rulers and leaders in so many places oppose a Christian witness and set their hand against freedom-loving democracies? This is the reality of a world that does not know Christ. It is the kind of world that compels us to go, undeterred by the threat, to confront a lost world with the claims of the One who is King of kings and Lord of lords.

But even in recognizing the hostility and threats they encountered—in a world where Jews and Gentiles, a Roman governor and pagan king had all conspired to put to death the Son of God—they acknowledged their confidence in a sovereign God. They reminded God that He was the one who created the earth and everything in it. And in response to the crucifixion of Jesus and the threats and dangers they now encountered, they confessed all that had happened was in accord with God's providence and purpose, that nothing had happened contrary to His predestined purpose (Acts 4:28).

We get our English word providence from two Latin words: "video," which means "to see," and the prefix "pro" which means "before." God is able to see beforehand all that is going to occur and in His sovereignty is able to plan a way it can be used for His purpose. How often we have quoted Romans 8:28 in times of adversity and trial, "And we know that God causes all things to work together for good to those who love God, to those who are called according to His purpose." Christians, and even missionaries, are not exempt

> "AND WE KNOW THAT GOD CAUSES ALL THINGS TO WORK TOGETHER FOR GOOD TO THOSE WHO LOVE GOD, TO THOSE WHO ARE CALLED ACCORDING TO HIS PURPOSE."

from accidents, illness, and tragedies, but these unexpected and undesired turns of events never take God by surprise. They are not indications that we have been abandoned by God or that God is not all-powerful and unable to deter the misfortune with which we may be confronted.

Just as God knew that Jesus would be rejected and crucified, and before the foundation of the world planned to use it to redeem a lost world, He knows beforehand all that is going to happen to us. He knew before that fatal morning of December 30, 2002, that three missionaries would be gunned down at the Jibla Baptist Hospital. He knew that Bill Hyde would be included among the victims in that terrorist bombing at the Davao City airport. He knew four Southern Baptist workers, excitedly initiating a humanitarian project in Iraq, would be killed on March 15, 2004. He knew these things would happen, and they became components of His master plan to be glorified among the nations.

Why did God allow Bill Koehn to serve the people of Yemen for 28 years, Martha Myers for 24 years and Kathy Gariety for 10 years? Was it not so that their witness and everything they did at Jibla Baptist Hospital would bear fruit as a result of their death? Bill Hyde gave his life for the people of the Philippines. God allowed him to coordinate training of almost 1,000 church planters just a few weeks before he died, and his devotion and sacrifice continue to inspire those who share the gospel there.

The final chapters have not been written. We do not know what God is going to do in Iraq, but we are confident God's kingdom will come to that country, and nothing has been allowed to occur that cannot be aligned with His purpose to be glorified among the people of Iraq and throughout the Arab world.

When Dayna Curry and Heather Mercer were arrested by the Taliban in Afghanistan, brought to trial, and threatened with death, Dayna wrote from prison, "We believe one of the reasons we are here is to motivate and awaken people to pray for this nation. I have seen more clearly in my time here what an exciting hour this world is in. ... Our Father is up to something great for this nation and we are excited to see what He will do. We will soon see His purpose and glory in this mad situation. May it be to glorify our Lord and reach this desperately lost nation." She had already reconciled herself to the possibility that she might die, but that wasn't the point. Whether she lived or died as a result of this chaotic and irrational situation, her confidence was that God's purpose would be fulfilled, and God would be glorified among the people of Afghanistan.

Interestingly, the New Testament believers who accepted the commission of their Lord to be His witnesses and disciple the nations did not pray that the threats and dangers would be removed. They did not ask for their comfort zone to be restored so that they could proclaim the gospel with immunity to danger. On the contrary, they recognized that their suffering was an opportunity for God to work through the mighty hand of Jesus. Their only request was that they might speak the Word of God with boldness and confidence. They concluded their prayer in Acts 4:29, "And now, Lord, take note of their threats, and grant that Your bond-servants may speak Your word with all confidence." Who would question, in retrospect, that the bold and confident witness of Stephen in his death probably stirred the heart of a young Pharisee named Saul whom God would use to change the world?

Just as believers in the first century were faithful to proclaim the gospel in the face of dangers and risks, so should we pray that God will give us boldness and confidence to confront a hostile world with the message that represents its only hope, trusting the powerful hand of Jesus to work through our witness. God knows the threats we face. He is well aware of the dangers and risks—and whether one of them will claim our life—but His purpose cannot be deterred.

We would think that the news of missionaries being killed would discourage other candidates from applying. Yet our Office of Mission Personnel is getting a growing number of inquiries from candidates surrendering for missionary service following the news of these incidents. A hospital administrator called, volunteering to take Bill Koehn's place. He said that he had served in the military in the Middle East and was fully aware of the dangers, but was ready to give his life. A host of volunteers emerged offering to assure a continuing ministry in Iraq when news spread that four workers there had been killed.

A college student wrote, "As a student studying to become a missionary, I, too, grieve as I read the news stories of the four who were slain as they lived and ministered among the Iraqi people. I have a deep love and passion to reach Muslims. This news has not kept me from my desire to go; it has only made my desire even greater. No matter what may happen, there are still those who have never heard the gospel. These deaths are not in vain! There are still others that are desiring to go despite the fact that there is danger. For me to live is Christ and to die is gain."

A 14-year-old student wrote, "I was shocked and moved by the news (of the missionaries who died in Iraq). I am an active youth in church but recently things have been going on in my complicated teenage life that made me question my faith. Hearing the testimonies of the love and sacrifice of these four martyrs made me realize that there is no way to life but through Jesus Christ. I was too scared to step out of my comfort zone and use my high school as a mission field, but now sacrificing everything to serve Christ in Iraq shows me that there is nothing in life if you do not know the grace and mercy of Jesus Christ our Lord. It made me realize that I want to give my life to Jesus as a sacrifice, just as these did in Iraq."

Missionary colleagues also were inspired to renew their commitment as all across the world they said, "I want to run the race to the finish. I, too, want to be found faithful."

In each of our orientation sessions for new missionaries, I make a series of presentations on spiritual warfare. We realize that missionaries are being sent into Satan's territory for the nations and cultures where Christ is not known. 1 John 5:19 says, "We know that we are of God, and that the whole world lies in the power of the evil one." The spiritual challenges they will face will not only be opposition, resistance, and danger, but illness, conflict, and discouragement—anything Satan can throw at them to thwart the advancement of God's kingdom and deprive Him of His glory among the nations.

There isn't space to review all that is covered in those three days of presentations, but one of the passages we use is Revelation 12:11. It describes the saints who overcame the accuser and won the victory. We are told, "And they overcame him because of the blood of the Lamb and because of the word of their testimony, and they did not love their life even when faced with death." Victory over sin and Satan has already been provided through the blood of Jesus Christ that was shed on the cross. The word of testimony or confession and witness of one's own faith assured their stance in that victory. But the capstone of victory that guaranteed they could not be touched by temptation, sin, carnal desires, worldly values, or selfish gratification was the fact that they did not love their own lives—even to the point of death.

And what could Satan do with that?

Jesus had already explained to His disciples that they could save their life only as they were willing to lose it for His sake. But one who tried to hold on to this life and all its values would be the one who would ultimately lose his life. In John 12:24-25, He used the analogy of a seed being planted in the ground: "… Unless a grain of wheat falls into the earth and dies, it remains alone; but if it dies, it bears much fruit. He who loves his life loses it, and he who hates his life in this world will keep it to life eternal." How sad and foolish that so many hold on to this life. They become as a seed, all alone, concerned about their own self-preservation. But those who give their lives and are willing to die are the ones who bear much fruit for the kingdom.

These passages came to mind as I was meeting with a large gathering of missionary personnel from East Asia a few weeks after the Yemen tragedy. I was still emotionally fragile after the sequence of memorial services and visiting personnel serving at the Jibla hospital. All week at this conference I had heard testimonies of churches that had been harassed, pastors who had been imprisoned, persecuted, and martyred. Yet the church continued to grow at a phenomenal pace. I heard how cities and people groups had seen an influx of believers following the death of a leader. It was not preplanned as I shared the testimony of those in Yemen who had given their lives and as I expounded on Revelation 12:11 in the context of what was happening in East Asia. I related how I had been impressed with the passion of their call, which so many had expressed, and their desire to see their assigned city or people group come to know the Lord. Then spontaneously I asked, "If God should choose to provide a breakthrough of the gospel and a harvest among your people, but it would require the shedding of your blood, the giving of your life, as it has among Chinese Christians, would you be willing to say, 'I will not hold on to my own life, even unto death, if it can mean the salvation of my people'?"

I expected a significant number to rise, but I was overwhelmed when the entire auditorium instantly stood! The next day one of the men in that group shared with me that as I spoke he began to quiver, sensing where I was going in my comments. He said, "I was holding my wife's hand, and when you asked if we would stand she squeezed my hand as I squeezed hers, and we stood." He went on, "For the first time since we have been on the field, we have been liberated from fear and have a boldness to do whatever it takes to reach our people."

Heather Mercer has written of living in total abandonment for Jesus from that Taliban prison in Afghanistan where she was constantly reminded that she was facing a possible death penalty for proselytizing. "I am learning every day what it means to love the Lord your God with all your heart, mind, soul, and strength," she reflected. "It is my desire that I would lay down whatever is to my profit and consider it loss for the sake of Christ my Lord. I'm learning what it means to be satisfied in the presence of Jesus Christ alone and to offer my life as a living sacrifice to Him."

It is unlikely that many—if any—of those missionaries in East Asia will be called to a martyr's crown. But a total commitment of one's life results in a passion and zeal that cannot be squelched. God will use those who do not love nor hold on to their own lives; they will be the ones to reach a lost world. They are the ones who discover the truth of what Martin Luther expressed as he wrote the fourth verse to his hymn, "A Mighty Fortress is Our God."

> *Let goods and kindred go,*
> *This mortal life also;*

The body they may kill,
God's truth abideth still;
His kingdom is forever.

I thought it ironic that the week I completed the writing of this volume, my wife and I took a few days of vacation in the Blue Ridge Mountains of Virginia. We included in our excursion a visit to Gettysburg, Pennsylvania. It was an impressive day touring the battlefield and being reminded of this tragic event in the history of our nation. Standing on the spot where President Lincoln delivered his famous Gettysburg address to dedicate the cemetery where thousands of soldiers were buried, I recalled the words that I had once memorized as a schoolboy.

Lincoln spoke of whether or not a nation conceived in liberty and dedicated to the proposition that all men are created equal could endure. In conclusion, he acknowledged that he could not dedicate the ground that had already been hallowed by those who shed blood there. Appropriately, he challenged the nation to be dedicated to the cause for which those who died gave their last full measure of devotion, "that these dead shall not have died in vain."

As I stood on that hallowed ground of Gettysburg where so many had died for the cause to which Lincoln spoke, I thought of these missionary martyrs who had given their full measure of devotion for the cause of Christ. I knew each of them personally, their love for the Lord, and their passion for reaching a lost world. I prayed that they would not have died in vain.

Lincoln expressed the concern that it remained to be seen whether or not the nation would endure. For us, it remains to be seen if the cause for which these died—the cause of global evange-lization—will be fulfilled by this generation. They died, not to pre-serve a nation, but that all peoples and nations would one day know and worship our Lord. May we who follow be found faithful that they would not have died in vain. May we give of ourselves with the same devotion to the unfinished task as those who testified by their blood that they loved not their own lives, even unto death.

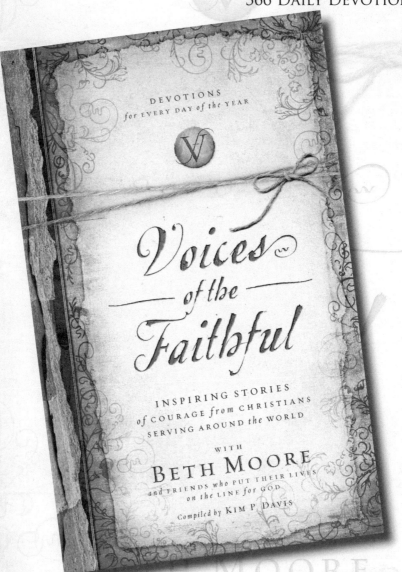

Also Available!

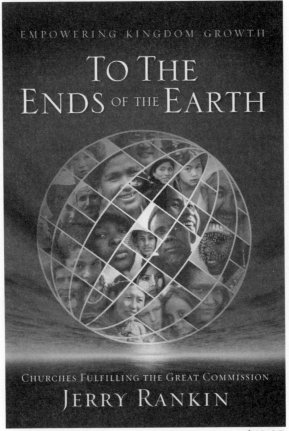

$19.95

Empowering Kingdom Growth:
To the Ends of the Earth
by Jerry Rankin

Empowering Kingdom Growth: To the Ends of the Earth is God's desire for all peoples and nations to worship Him. Fulfilling God's desire takes prayer, alignment with His purpose, change of priority, strategic witness and committed partners. Read along as Jerry Rankin, president of the International Mission Board, shares his perspectives on global evangelization and how churches can fulfill the Great Commission.

Order at **http://resources.imb.org** *or call (800) 999-3113.*